# Scottish
## Canyons

Danny Watts

 **Pesda Press** LTD

www.pesdapress.com

First published in Great Britain 2021 by Pesda Press
Tan y Coed Canol
Ceunant
Caernarfon
Gwynedd
LL55 4RN

© Copyright 2021    Danny Watts

Maps – Bute Cartographic
Contains Ordnance Survey data © Crown copyright and database right 2021

ISBN:   978-1-906095-79-6

Printed and bound in Poland. www.lfbookservices.co.uk

# Foreword

As kayaking developed in Scotland in the early 90s, the hunt for steeper rivers began. The race was on to get as many first descents as possible, ticking off new waterfalls or steep-sided gorges hidden all over Scotland, but as kayakers started to explore into tighter and steeper rivers, we found ourselves starting to abseil sections of rivers and lower our boats down. Eventually there were rivers that were left untamed by a kayak, and so began the sport of canyoning in Scotland.

Of course, research was a lot harder back then. Without the luxury of the internet most rivers were found by OS map and then scouted on foot. This new sport of canyoning allowed us to access steeper more remote canyons, enjoying the pioneering feel of it all, discovering the thrill of another new jump or slide hidden away. Canyoning in Scotland has developed a lot since then, as it has around the world. We only started adding infrastructure into the canyons of Scotland in the year 2000, helping to make them more accessible for people to explore the variety of canyons Scotland has to offer.

Thankfully, Danny has now made an amazing job of collecting all the information for this guidebook, I hope you enjoy it and the experiences canyoning will bring you.

Rig and rap safe! – Ben Starkie.

📷 Ben Starkie – Photo: Nadi Khan

# Acknowledgements

A huge thank you must go to my friends over the years who have joined me all around Scotland to descend these cold canyons and collect information to help bring this guidebook to fruition – Gavin Branter, Mathew Burden, Michael Aylen, Jessica Acheson, Bryony Brooks, Scott Gibson, Mitch Craig, Steve McNeil, Intrepidus and many more.

A special thank you to Ben Starkie, Olly Baylis, Andy Taylor, Rhian Anthony, and John Stewart, for all their help in creating this guidebook.

Also, thanks to Mum & Gal for all their help over the years in many ways.

Finally, the biggest thank you to Ellie Raymond for her amazing patience and support while I would not stop talking about canyoning.

## Photographic acknowledgements

Photos are by the author except where acknowledged in the captions. A special thanks to The Adventure Photographers for their spectacular photographs of so many of the canyons.

# Contents

Big jump (Route 34)
- The Adventure Photographers

# Introduction

Scotland, a country famously known for the beautiful highlands, its delicious single malt whisky and, of course, the 'dreich' weather. There are many outdoor activities that can be pursued, from rock climbing and hiking in the mountains to kayaking in the rivers or around the coastline. The sport of canyoning, however, is relatively new here and its development has been hindered, until now, by the lack of a guidebook.

This guidebook has been created for both experienced canyoneers and for those who have just started to delve into this adventurous sport. Here you will find information about some of the best canyons and gorges Scotland has to offer. There are 47 Scottish routes to explore, ranging from beautiful entry-level gorge-walks to committing and challenging canyon descents. Each route has been placed into one of four regions:

Far North & Isles, West Coast, Central and Southern.

*"In Scotland there is no such thing as bad weather –*
*Only the wrong clothes." – Billy Connolly*

# What is Canyoning?

Have you ever been out hiking in the mountains and seen a series of beautiful waterfalls disappearing into a steep sided-gorge and wondered "What's down there?"

This is where 'Canyoning' comes in!

Canyoning is an adventurous sport that follows the path of a stream down the mountain side – usually in steep-sided gorges, through cold plunge pools and over tumbling waterfalls. This extreme sport requires a combined range of skills to overcome the obstacles along the river path; from abseiling to jumping, scrambling, climbing, sliding, and swimming. When you put all of this together, it enables you to explore a harsh yet outstanding environment where few have ever been before.

Of course, all of this can make canyoning an extremely dangerous activity and should not be something you just 'have a go at'! As with climbing or caving, if you are new to the sport, you should seek advice and training from professionals first. In the UK, you can look to the UKCA (UK Canyoning Association) for training courses throughout the year on www.ukcanyoning.org. They offer introductory lessons that help you begin your journey into the sport of canyoning, or more advanced courses for the experienced canyoneer wanting to tackle harder canyons in Scotland or abroad. You may also want to check out the V7 Academy which has in-depth online training videos on www.v7academy.com – a great place to start learning the basics to the sport of canyoning and develop more advanced techniques.

The canyoning season in Scotland can theoretically be all year round, but a lot of people may choose to refrain from descending into ice-cold waterfalls and brain-freezing plunge pools in the depths of winter, and I don't blame them. So, with that said, the best months for canyoning in Scotland are from April to October.

# Warning – Canyoning is a Dangerous Activity

The canyon routes detailed in this guidebook are intended for the use of an experienced audience; either dedicated canyoneers or outdoor enthusiasts with transferable skills. Canyoning comes with very real risks which often relate specifically to the sport. Practicing safe canyoning requires you to have good judgment based on your personal skills and a realistic understanding of your experience and limitations before choosing to descend any route. Even those with many years' experience in mountaineering or rock-climbing should assess their skill-set before descending canyon routes as many techniques used in canyoning are specific to the sport and not used elsewhere.

Hazards within a canyon can change constantly, and this guidebook cannot keep you safe from these dangers. Over time, anchors for abseils can become damaged or removed by floods and snowmelt, deep pools can fill up with debris or silt from a storm or landslides, hydroelectric dams can be built which can change the flow of the canyon or cause flash flooding. With this knowledge, you must always be prepared for these changes and learn the skills to overcome any new circumstances.

There is no substitute for undertaking a training course in canyoning to learn the necessary skills required to safely descend these routes. An introduction to the risks of the sport and basic techniques used can be seen in the 'Flash Flood Awareness', 'Safety and Planning', 'Equipment' and 'Techniques' sections at the beginning of the book.

## Emergency contacts

In case of an emergency, call 999 and ask for the Police then Mountain Rescue.

### Important notice

Although great care has been taken by the author to ensure all information contained within this book is as accurate as possible at the time of writing, the author and Pesda Press do not take any responsibility in connection with the use of the information given in this guidebook. It is your own personal decision as to whether to descend a gorge / canyon or not.

# How to Use this Guidebook

This guidebook includes some of the best canyoning routes that have been discovered and explored within Scotland.

## Star rating

As you look through the different canyons and gorges detailed, you will see a star rating given to each route. While every route has its own merits, the use of a 4-star rating system helps to distinguish the difference in quality. This rating system considers the natural beauty of the canyon and the level of thrill it may offer with a normal level of water, but as always, assessing quality comes down to a matter of opinion and these ratings are only a guide.

## Grade

The grade given to each canyon route is based on the hardest section(s) of the canyon with a normal level of water. This is always subject to change; higher water levels can create different hazards or anchors could be missing which may create a difficult rigging situation.

## Location

Each canyon route has been named by the first team to descend it, but the river itself has a name; it's mentioned on each route so you can double check you are in the right place. Map coordinates have also been given to mark the start and end of each canyoning route. These are given as Grid References for use with OS maps and Latitude and Longitude to 4 decimal points which should work with any GPS system.

## Timings

There is an approach, descent and return time given with each route. These times are only estimates, based on a team of four competent canyoneers who have not descended the route before. An approximate canyon length is also detailed to give you an idea of the size of the route. These pieces of information will help you to plan your trip accordingly and to avoid any major surprises.

## Abseil length

You will also see that the longest abseil is noted on each route. With this information you can assess the rope lengths required for each canyon, but be sure to check each description in more detail as there may be variations. The length given is only an approximation and is not an exact measurement.

## Reading the topographic maps

Topos are a simplified graphical cross-section of a canyon that highlight the main features of the route. There are a number of topos in this guidebook to help you understand what you will find on specific routes. Not all routes in this book have a topographic map; this may be because of the simpler nature of the given route or because the majority of the route involves gorge-walking with only a few key features that will be mentioned in the description.

Using the symbols located on the legend given on the inside back cover, you will be able to read these topographic maps and gain a better understanding of what you will encounter when descending the canyon route.

### Please note

Only the main features of the canyon have been included on the topos. During the sections of gorge-walking you may still discover unmapped features that you will be required to navigate under your own judgement. Canyons are constantly changing; you should always check landing pools for debris and depth before jumping or tobogganing to prevent any serious injuries.

### Helpful tip

If you are carrying a waterproof digital camera into the canyon, you should take photos of the canyon route and maps from this book to have as a reference on your approach and during your descent.

# Canyon Grading System

Canyoning in the UK has its own grading system to help you to judge the difficulty of the descent and enable you to prepare yourself accordingly for the journey.

This guidebook uses an extended version of the current UKCA canyon grading system, which is made up of two figures. The first figure is numeric, relating to the terrain and rope-work involved to safely descend the canyon. The second figure is an alphabet character, relating to the volume of water and strength of current. The canyons are graded on the basis of the most difficult section(s) of the descent.

## Technical rope work

**1** Non-technical; no rope required. This gorge may involve some easy scrambling and downclimbing. It is usually possible to travel both up and down the river. Easy to exit at any point.

**2** Steeper terrain involving near vertical scrambling or climbing. Handlines or belays may be required. Rope recommended. Exits may be fewer.

**3** Basic canyoning involving simple abseils. Exposed waterfalls that are too dangerous to downclimb. Rope and rigging gear is required. Single-pitch abseils with obvious natural anchors or bolts. Escape possible after each rappel.

**3+** Single-pitch abseils with more complicated anchors or marginal anchors. Handlines may be required to access the abseil pitch-head. Harder to escape, may require basic climbing.

**4** Advanced canyoning involving one or more of the following skills: multi-pitch abseils, guided rappels, obscure anchor building or handlines with intermediate points. Bolting and rigging gear recommended. Exits may be very few and escape can be difficult.

**4+** Multiple advanced canyoning skills required to safely descend. Added difficulties may include deviations, strong whistle communication, lead / aid climbing or obligatory jumps. Bolting, rigging, and rescue kit necessary. May be extremely difficult to escape from.

**5** Advanced canyoning with a committing descent and almost no escape. Anchor building and rope work will be difficult, complex, or marginal. Bolting, rigging and rescue kit necessary. The canyon may also be remote, and any rescue will prove to be difficult.

## Aquatic nature

**A**   Normally has water but with little to almost no flow. Water hazards may be non-existent.

**B**   Water flow with a stronger current, abseils may be aquatic in nature. Some small hazards may be created in the water path. Swimming ability required.

**C**   Strong currents in the river creating dangerous hydraulics and hazards. Strong swimming ability required. Some abseils will be very aquatic.

**D**   Extreme hazards created in the canyon by a strong current. Dangerous hydraulics that will be difficult to overcome and involve advanced skills. Experienced canyoneers only.

### Water levels warning

The water levels in canyons can fluctuate greatly in Scotland, from season to season or even day to day. If you arrive at a canyon and discover the water level to be greater than anticipated, it should be assumed that the descent will be far more difficult than the grade it was given. Please re-evaluate your decision to attempt the descent or choose a more suitable canyon where possible.

# Safety and Etiquette

Before you enter a canyon or gorge, you should consider these 10 golden rules to help practise safe canyoning and to improve the image of canyoning in Scotland.

## Safety

- Prepare for the canyon to be harder than described and carry extra rope.

- Look at multiple weather forecasts.

- Plan for any emergencies by carrying a first aid kit and always let someone know where you are going and when they should expect you back.

- Always carry anchor building equipment. Abseil anchors may be damaged or missing.

- If you have a waterproof camera, take photos of the canyon route in this guide to have on hand as a reference while descending.

- Know the limits of your team members and choose a suitable route.

## Etiquette

- Do not obstruct any gates or roads when parking your car. Although there is a 'right to roam' act in Scotland, be respectful of private land.

- Respect the mountain and its users. Take your rubbish home; if you can carry it in, you can carry it out!

- When changing, try to stay respectful. Nobody wants to see a cold naked canyoneer!

- Help out local communities by purchasing a beverage at a pub or café afterwards. It would be greatly appreciated, and help spread a positive image of canyoneers in Scotland.

These are only guidelines we have created to help you get out there and explore these amazing locations, all while staying safe and helping us develop the growing sport of canyoning within Scotland and the rest of the UK.

# Communication

Communication is key! In the canyoning environment you are going to find it hard to communicate by voice as the waterfalls rumble loudly around you. Instead, we use simple hand signals when line of sight is possible, and whistle signals for when it is not. Below is a basic summary of some of the signals we use as canyon guides, but it's important to have a system that works between you and your team members.

## Whistle signals

Here is a summary of some simple whistle communications you can use when canyoning. To ensure you give the correct whistle command, try to clear out any water that may reside in your whistle before using it (try sucking out any water first).

> 1 Blast – STOP
>
> 2 Blasts – OFF ROPE / OK
>
> 3 Blasts – NEED MORE ROPE
>
> Repeated Blasts – EMERGENCY

## Hand signals

OK                              Stop

Need the bag

Take in rope

Lower the rope

Guided rappel

First aid

# Equipment

Before you descend into these wet and dangerous canyons / gorges, you're going to need some equipment. There are two sections to this:

**Personal equipment** – the kit that is worn and carried on your person.

**Group equipment** – the kit that is carried in a canyoning bag between you.

## Personal equipment

📷 Personal equipment

**Wetsuit** – The rivers of Scotland are cold, and hypothermia is a real risk when you immerse yourself for long periods of time in these waters. Having a correctly fitting wetsuit is essential and the thickness of the suit can make all the difference. A 3mm suit should suffice in the summer months, but a 5mm option is the optimal choice to extend your canyoning season. There are many choices out there and there are wetsuits designed specifically for the sport of canyoning, but the most common choice is a surfing wetsuit. A surfing wetsuit is an adequate option, but they can be prone to abrasion and tearing in the rough canyon environment.

**Footwear** – Investing in a pair of specialist canyoning shoes can make an incredible difference to your journey in the canyon, but they are not an absolute essential. An old pair of trainers will do the job. However, they lack ankle support while clambering on slippery rock. Hiking boots are a bad option as they offer next-to-no grip due to their stiff soles. But whatever you wear, neoprene socks are a must to keep your feet warm.

**Helmet** – There is always the risk of a head injury while in a gorge, so a helmet should be worn at all times during your descent. The decision is yours as to whether you choose to wear a white water helmet or climbing helmet. There are arguments for either option; it is important to learn and understand the different type of protection each one offers, this will help you to decide what helmet to wear while canyoning.

**Buoyancy aid** – Many canyoneers in the UK choose not to wear a buoyancy aid while canyoning, and many choose to always wear one. (Bear in mind that a canyoning wetsuit will offer some bouyancy in itself.) Wearing a buoyancy aid may offer peace of mind in white-water elements but they may adversely affect your ability to swim and generally make it difficult to see your harness, leaving room for error when clipping into abseils. It is a personal preference whether to wear a buoyancy aid or not.

**Harness** – Any climbing harness will do for a canyon descent provided it fits you correctly over a wetsuit. Again, there are specialist harnesses on the market for canyoning and these will become essential as you delve into more advanced canyons. These canyoning harnesses will come with a protective seat which saves your wetsuit and harness from wear & tear. Always check for signs of damage before using your harness.

**Descender** – The Petzl Piranha is the number one choice for an abseil device in canyoning. It has additional features allowing you to increase friction while descending if required for any reason. There are other options; even the simple figure-of-eight is a great choice. Whatever device you choose, it is essential that you understand how to use your descender correctly and safely.

**Karabiners** – It is essential to have a few spare locking karabiners on your harness. They will have many uses during a canyoning trip – just make sure you maintain them well, as the watery environment will take its toll on their functionality.

**Lanyards** – These are crucial for clipping into anchors near exposed edges or onto handlines while traversing. You can purchase ready-made lanyards from climbing stores, but lanyards can easily be made from a length of 9 or 10mm dynamic rope. It can be helpful to have one lanyard shorter than the other but make sure the long one remains within arm's length.

**Figure-of-eight** – A classic piece of equipment used in mountaineering, climbing, caving and now canyoning. Usually kept on a quickdraw made up of two locking karabiners instead of snap-gates. It is mainly used for rigging releasable abseils but is also handy as a back-up descender.

**Knife** – Used only in emergencies when it comes to rope work, except for cutting webbing when building anchors. There are harness mounting options or folding knives that can clip onto a karabiner.

**Whistle** – Entering a canyon without this little life-saver is going to make communicating difficult. The loud canyon environment can make it impossible to communicate between team members. Using simple whistle signals can help. The type of whistle, however, is especially important. The normal low-pitched hillwalking whistle is almost impossible to hear over the rumble of waterfalls. Instead opt for a high-pitched bean-less whistle like the Fox 40.

## Group equipment

📷 Group equipment

**Canyon bag** – A strong PVC bag with multiple drainage holes is an essential piece of equipment. Without adequate drainage, the bag can fill with water and become extremely heavy as you abseil down with it attached to you. Canyoning bags are robustly built for the harsh environment of the canyon. Some have built in floatation but not all, so you may need to attach some foam or an empty bottle at the base of your bag to stop it from sinking.

**Rope** – There are numerous choices of rope on the market, but you will need to understand the different types as only a few are suitable for canyoning. Generally speaking, semi-static ropes are the best option for the canyon environment and having one that is brightly coloured can be extremely helpful. You will also find that some float and some do not, so it is a matter of preference as to which type of rope you choose.

**First aid kit** – Essential for any outdoor activity and you shouldn't leave home without one. What you carry in your first aid kit is up to you but having the knowledge to use what you are carrying is important to effectively provide first aid. A few items that a canyoneer may carry on top of a standard kit include; glucose gel, a SAM splint, a blizzard blanket and an elastic cohesive bandage. (The latter is a bandage wrap used on horses that sticks to itself – ideal in a wet environment when adhesion becomes difficult).

**Waterproof case** – Whether a barrel or a box, you need a container that can keep your first aid, food and phone dry. A good-sized barrel at the bottom of the canyon bag also acts as a float. It is still a good idea to seal anything inside a barrel in a dry bag in case the barrel leaks.

**Food / water** – Luckily, most of the canyons in Scotland have delicious drinkable water, but this isn't always the case. Low lying gorges, or routes with dams on them may not be suitable to drink from, and so it is best to carry a bottle of water. Pack some food to keep your energy levels up. High sugar chocolate bars or trail mix usually go down well.

**Goggles** – Quite the essential piece of equipment. They are important when checking the depths of pools and underwater hazards before somebody jumps in. Inevitably someone is going to drop something at some point, which will require some diving to retrieve the item.

**Emergency phone** – Either your phone or an old back-up phone, sealed in a dry bag. You might not always get signal in a canyon, but you may be able to escape and call for help. Just make sure it's charged.

## Rigging equipment

Before a waterfall can be abseiled, an anchor must be built. There are many different types of anchors that can be found in a canyon, and there are many methods to rig an anchor. After training and learning how to build canyoning anchors safely you will most likely carry lengths of webbing and maillons suitable for rigging anchors and abseiling. As you venture into more advanced canyons, the equipment you carry may extend to hand-drills, bolts and pitons.

# Techniques

The following sections on canyoning techniques are described only in basic detail. It is assumed that the reader is already aware of these techniques and has proficient knowledge of when and how to use these skills. This information should only be used as a supplement to an already competent canyoneer.

Canyoning is a sport that combines many different techniques, most of which have been developed from other outdoor pursuits to better suit the canyoning environment. However, there are techniques unique to the sport.

Gorge Walking

## Moving in a canyon

Probably the most care demanding thing you will ever do is clamber over the wet, algae-covered rocks that you will find in every single canyon! The slippery nature of all gorges and canyons makes them an accident-prone environment, if you choose to walk about carelessly. It is better to move slowly and keep low to the ground with hands-on-rock so you can catch yourself if you do slip.

## Downclimbing and spotting

Some features in the canyon can be navigated by simply climbing down. The decision as to whether or not to rig an abseil instead should be based on the skill of the team.

◎ Spotting

When downclimbing any feature you may find yourself using a variety of techniques. You might sit down and utilise the friction of the harness protection pad to shuffle down, or in narrow sections you may use a technique called bridging. Whichever technique you use it is always best practice to spot and protect members of the team to help avoid injuries. You can do this by getting into a secure spot where you can extend a hand towards them and stop them from falling further if they slip. Never hesitate to accept or offer help to team members.

## Bridging

Bridging is an advanced technique where you use opposing forces on opposite walls to span a gap over the river. Using your hands, feet, knees, back or anything that adds friction on rocks, you can navigate along / down the narrow section, generally having to keep your feet in a high position.

Bridging

## Tobogganing

Tobogganing in a canyon has to be, in my opinion, the highlight of the sport. It is the art of sliding down a rockface that has been smoothed by the erosive force of water. It is crucial, however, to make an assessment of the toboggan first; checking the sliding surface for protruding features or breaks in the rockface, checking the pool for hazards such as obstacles or hydraulics. When tobogganing, your body position is important. The safest method is to lay flat on your back with your feet together and pointing downstream, keeping your arms straight and placed in front of you to keep your elbows protected from impact. Try to let your muscles relax as you slide down the toboggan; if your body is stiff it is likely that you will feel every bump.

Tobogganing

## Jumping

For most, this is the biggest thrill in the sport of canyoning, but it is also the main cause of injuries sustained while canyoning. You should always check the depth of a pool and look for any underwater hazards (debris, rocks, shelves, etc.) before jumping in. You can do this by diving down, wearing a good set of goggles, to observe the landing zone. Jumping sounds simple but improper technique can cause serious injury. Confidently execute your jump, making sure you have a solid, grippy stance first before taking off with one foot leading the momentum. In the air, on larger jumps, you will need to balance yourself by using your arms to keep your body in an upright position. Upon impact with the water; make sure your feet are together with a slight bend in your knees, your arms are tucked in across your chest, look straight ahead and not down at the water and of course, take a deep breath before you take the plunge.

Jumping

## Abseiling (aka rappelling)

Not every abseil in a canyon will be in the flow of water but having an adapted technique for when they are is important. It can be intimidating to abseil into a rushing waterfall but remember to take your time, don't try to rush down the pitch as this can lead to mistakes. Unlike abseiling down a dry cliff, you won't always remain on your feet while walking down the rockface of the waterfall as it will inherently be slippery. Instead, you need to be more dynamic by using your knees or even abseiling while sliding down on your side. Using extra friction on your descender will help you maintain control of your speed during descent, especially if you are carrying any bags clipped to your harness. (Be careful wearing a bag on your back when abseiling in the flow as you could get inverted!)

Abseiling into the flow

Sometimes you may find an abseil that has a turbulent pool of water at its base. There are a few techniques that should be used to avoid any rope entanglements while in white water. Make sure the end of the rope is free of any knots and abseil without the use of any Prusiks. Consider throwing or zip-lining any bags downstream before dropping into the water, making sure there is someone downstream to receive these. Try to set the rope length just off of the top of the pool so that you are not encumbered by a mess of rope as you try to swim away from the hazard. Where possible, use a guided rappel to save most of the team from having to navigate the hazard.

[📷] Guided rappel

# Flash Flood Awareness

Before descending into any kind of canyon or gorge terrain it is of the utmost importance to be aware of the dangers of flash flooding. Knowing what, why, and when flash floods may occur can help you make the best judgements to prevent serious injury or worse.

### What is a flash flood?

Flash flooding is when a river dramatically increases in volume and current in the space of only a few minutes or even seconds! This phenomenon is much more likely to occur in a canyoning environment than in open rivers.

### How does a flash flood occur?

Most canyons and gorges are formed at the base of a large catchment area of a river. It is here that the volume of water squeezes its way through a steep-sided river, like water flowing through the spout of a funnel. Unlike the open rivers, where the volume of water can burst the banks and overflow into the surrounding area, the steep terrain of a canyon traps this water in. This effect forces the river to rise rapidly in height and has been known, in more dramatic cases, to make a wall of water as it rushes through the canyon.

### When does a flash flood happen?

The most common cause of flash flooding is the weather. Hydroelectric dams are another common cause, due to their capacity to release large amounts of water in a short space of time. There are a variety of different dams in Scotland and it is important to understand the different dangers presented by each one. Other causes of flash floods are natural dams created by storms and debris that could break without warning – releasing a surge of water into the canyon.

### What checks should be made before a descent?

The weather! Keep an eye on the weather a week before your planned trip. If it has been raining all week and the ground is well saturated, it won't take much rain for the river to rise. Before heading out to the canyon you should check multiple weather forecasts to get a well-rounded idea of what the weather may do that day.

The other important item to check is the catchment area of the river. You can do this by looking at OS maps to see what is above the canyon. Some points to consider are: How big is the catchment area? What is the gradient? Is there a hydro scheme? Are there trees or is the terrain of the catchment boggy? All of these points and more will help you to have a better understanding of the likelihood of a flash flood occurring within a specific canyon.

## Warning signs

In the unfortunate event you are caught in a canyon when a flash flood occurs there may be some tell-tale signs to warn you of the impending danger.

**Heavy rainfall** – a strong indicator that the river volume may increase.

**Sound** – is it getting harder to hear over the rumbling of the water?

**Debris and water colour** – the river may change colour as debris and silt is washed in from the sides by rising waters.

**Smell** – a strange indicator, but you will notice a change in scents as the waters start to rise.

## What to do in a flash flood?

Do not try to outrun a flash flood!

Seek higher ground or escape the canyon if possible.

Find a protected area (i.e. behind a waterfall, in the eddy of a large boulder) and wait it out.

**Defensive swimming** – only as the last resort if you are caught in the flow and heading downstream!

### Defensive swimming

This is a protected position adopted while floating downstream; lying flat on your back and as close to the surface as possible with your feet facing down-stream, arms out to the sides using the backstroke to navigate your direction.

[◎] In deep (Route 3) - The Adventure Photographers

# Far North & Isles

Arguably the best place to go to enjoy a day or two of adventure canyoning. In the North you'll find some of the biggest canyons and gorges to sink your teeth into, some of which consist of a different rock type to most of the Scottish canyons. The Isle of Skye of course has the famous 'Fairy Pools' which are worth a visit for some fun. Or if you're on Mull, have a dip in the short but beautiful Ben More Canyon.

# Pharaoh's Canyon – Upper

| | |
|---|---|
| **Star rating** | ★★★★ |
| **Grade** | 4 B/C |
| **River** | Allt Airdeasaidh |
| **Duration** | 45mins approach – 2hrs descent – return via Lower Section |
| **Canyon length** | 500m |
| **Longest abseil** | 27m |
| **Parking** | NH 051 896   (57.8536, -5.2858) |
| **In** | NH 048 888   (57.8465, -5.2908) |
| **Out** | NH 051 893   (57.8502, -5.2865) |

## Canyon description

One magnificent canyon, tucked away in the north of Scotland. Made up of sandstone, it has a brilliant grippy nature – unlike all the others! It breaks down into two parts, the upper being the deep canyon full of large waterfalls and the lower part known as the 'Pharaoh's Playground'. Go find out why.

## Getting there

Following the same directions as for Dundonnell Canyon (Route 3), keep driving past Dundonnell Canyon towards Dundonnell village. Continue on the A832 for another 2.5 miles to the hamlet of Ardessie. A bridge over the bottom of the canyon gives you a view of the final waterfall. Park in a large layby on the left by a green pump house.

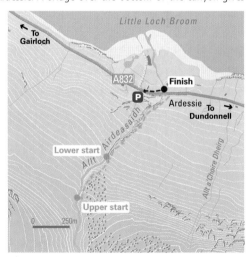

## Approach

Walk back towards the canyon and follow a path up, on river-right. You will be able to view the lower section as you walk up next to it and sometimes on the side of it. Keep following the path up the hill as it gets steeper and the river

**1**

disappears from sight. When you reach a bunch of boulders at the top of the path, start to make your way down to the river and get in where it's easiest to access.

## Descent

Make your way down a downclimb / shallow jump and towards the first big waterfall. Carefully climb out to the left to find a chockstone anchor to rig for the starting abseil. Another shorter abseil then leads you to the next big pitch. At the top of this next waterfall there are signs of rockfall, take care here. This 27m pitch can be rather aquatic towards the bottom as the water crashes overhead, a thrilling experience. Grippy gorge-walking and a couple of abseils lead you down through this beautiful gorge until you reach the final two waterfalls in the upper section. The first is another mildly aquatic abseil from the right, the next has anchors around to the left just over a ledge. All that remains is some beautiful gorge-walking out the upper section onto an open plateau where the 'playground' begins.

## Water level marker

You can view the last rappel of the lower section from the road bridge. It will go in higher water levels as most abseils can be done out of the flow, but a few will give you a kicking. The waterfall by the road will look quite substantial but that is a good medium level. If it's solid white, then it's very high.

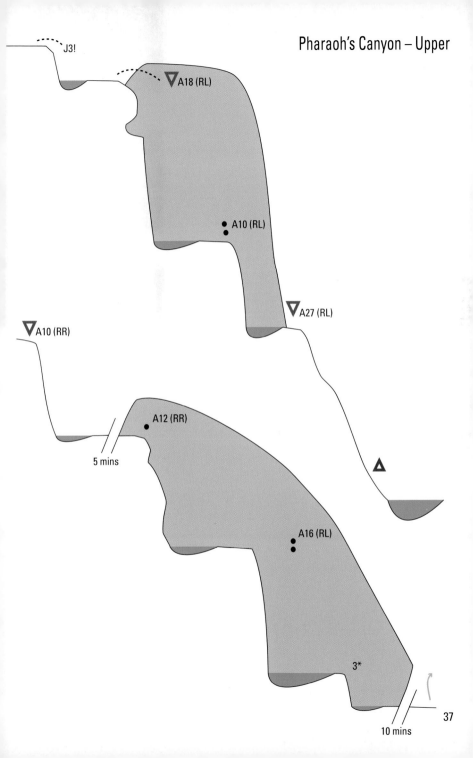

# Pharaoh's Canyon – Lower

| | |
|---|---|
| **Star rating** | ★★★ |
| **Grade** | 4 B |
| **River** | Allt Airdeasaidh |
| **Duration** | 30mins approach – 1hr 30mins descent – 5mins return |
| **Canyon length** | 450m |
| **Longest abseil** | 20m |
| **Parking** | NH 051 896   (57.8536, -5.2858) |
| **In** | NH 051 893   (57.8502, -5.2865) |
| **Out** | NH 054 896   (57.8533, -5.2812) |

## Canyon description

The 'Pharaoh's Playground', as it is also known, is the open plateau, lower section of the canyon where you can explore multiple routes down the river. The start falls down into a side gorge before opening out to glorious views over Little Loch Broom.

## Getting there

See directions under Pharaoh's Canyon – Upper.

## Approach

Follow the same route up for the Upper section of the canyon but stop on a large plateau of sandstone where the river emerges from a steep-sided gorge. You should see a big blue pipe in the river which directs some flow to the pump house.

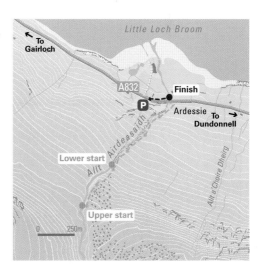

## Descent

On this large plateau you will see the water flow

📷 Side gorge – The Adventure Photographe

**2**

drops back down into a side-gorge, an awkward abseil gives you access into it but this gorge can be avoided by walking down river-right if you so choose. There are a few features to overcome in here, finishing with a small abseil at the end. After this short gorge section, the open area is yours to pick and choose your way down; there are some fun features to be found. The large falls in the middle of this, offers a large but technical jump (technical because of a tight landing area), be careful and inspect first. You'll also find a boulder suspended over a gorge which has been jumped from but there is an underwater ledge and it is a bit shallow!

When you reach the final waterfall by the road, you have two options for an abseil. Either take the aquatic option from a tree anchor river-left or a dry abseil from bolts at a lower point river-right. You can now exit here onto the bridge or take the climb under the road bridge first. Walk back along the road to the car.

**Water level marker**

See details under Pharaoh's Canyon – Upper.

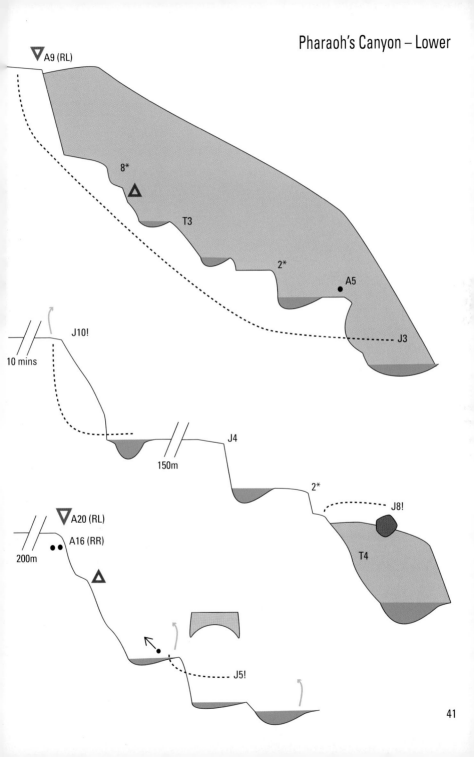

📷 No easy escape

# Dundonnell Canyon

| Star rating | ★★★★ |
|---|---|
| Grade | 4+ B/C |
| River | Dundonnell River |
| Duration | 10mins approach – 2 to 3hrs descent – 15mins return |
| Canyon length | 850m |
| Longest abseil | 18m |
| Parking | NH 128 842  (57.8080, -5.1524) |
| In | NH 126 844  (57.8098, -5.1560) |
| Out | NH 119 847  (57.8129, -5.1681) |

## Canyon description

A magnificent slot canyon in the far north of Scotland. It's right beside the road yet unseen by anyone passing by. This is a committing descent into a canyon full of deep peaty pools and outstanding carved walls.

## Getting there

Drive along the A835 from Inverness towards Ullapool until you reach the Corrieshalloch Gorge. Turn left here down the A832 to Dundonnell. After about 10mins on the A832, the road starts to lead downhill and turns left as the steep glen takes a turn. There is a layby on the right just after the road bends left. There should be a path down to a firepit near the river-side if you are in the correct layby. Park here.

## Approach

Start walking downhill on the road. After no more than 5mins of walking, the river should start to disappear from sight. Start to walk down to the river and find an easy get in before the riverbanks get too steep. If the entry is steep, you've gone too far.

[○] Beautifully carved walls – The Adventure Photographers

## Descent

Drop into the river and start swimming downstream. The first feature should be two small drops which can be avoided by escaping up right and jumping off the riverbank into the large deep pool (check first). After a long swim you will arrive at the point of no return where a variety of options will commit you into the canyon.

Next you'll find a tricky section with two hidden siphons in the path of the waterfall. A traverse on bolts out right avoids these and you can then abseil down and around the corner, before the final drop, to a good ledge and a chain hanger. Abseil or possible big jump. Continuing down you'll pass the one point of escape, up a steep green gully river-left, before the canyon walls close in again. The next tight section can be taken direct in low water or a long traverse out right in high water. Following this, passing the tributary river, climb up to an awesome free hanging abseil.

A long swim leads to your exit in an amphitheatre of rock. Climb up river-left and then walk straight through the trees and back to the road. Walk back up the road to the car.

## Water level marker

As you are driving down the A832 on your approach to the canyon it is best to check the flow from the river upstream of the canyon. When the road starts to descend, some waterfalls will come into view on your right. Park in a layby to assess the flow. For Dundonnell canyon to be safe to enter - these waterfalls should look very low in volume and the river look rocky with only a gentle flow. Any more and the tight space in the canyon can create dangerous hydraulics. It's always best to explore this canyon after a good dry spell.

# Dundonnell Canyon

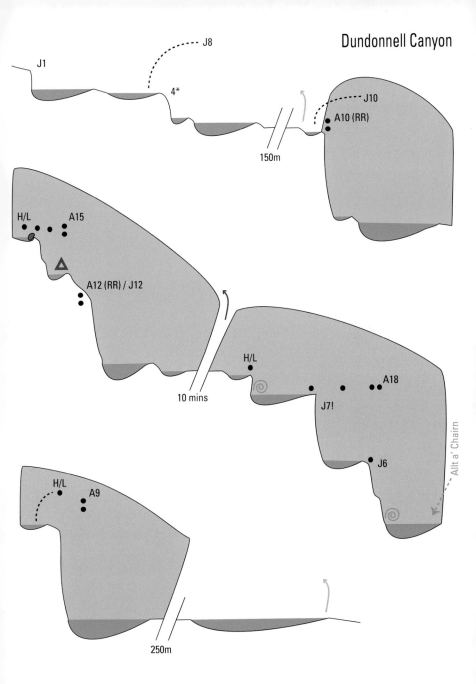

J1

J8

4*

150m

J10

A10 (RR)

H/L    A15

A12 (RR) / J12

10 mins

H/L

A18

J7!

J6

Allt a' Chairn

H/L    A9

250m

# Strone Gorge

| | |
|---|---|
| **Star rating** | ★★★ |
| **Grade** | 5 B/C |
| **River** | Abhainn Cuileig |
| **Duration** | 20mins approach – 3 to 4hrs descent – 30mins return |
| **Canyon length** | 2.6km |
| **Longest abseil** | 25m |
| **Parking** | NH 181 770 (57.7455, -5.0577) |
| **In** | NH 180 769 (57.7447, -5.0592) |
| **Out** | NH 192 789 (57.7637, -5.0408) |

## Canyon description

One of the longest canyon descents in Scotland that descends deeply into an awe-inspiring gorge. While mostly an epic gorge-walk there are still a few challenges to tackle, with one waterfall in particular that may be anchorless!

**Note** – There is no topo for this canyon as the features are very spread out and this particular route has had very few visitors. The canyon grade may decrease to 4+ B/C when the bolt situation is remedied.

## Getting there

Drive towards Ullapool on the A835 from Inverness. Before you reach Ullapool, you will get to Corrieshalloch Gorge. Take a left here along the A832 towards Dundonnell. Not far along this road is a viewpoint car park on the right overlooking the glen towards Ullapool; drive past this and park in a layby on the right, closer to the canyon start.

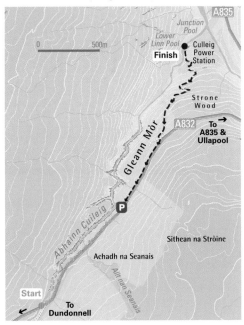

**4**

47

## Approach

Begin walking down the road in the direction towards Dundonnell. You will reach the road bridge over the canyon; get in downstream of this.

## Descent

The canyon begins with an aquatic abseil which commits you into the gorge. Deep pools and small down-climbable waterfalls lead through a beautiful broken-rock gorge. Eventually you will reach the committing main waterfall section of the canyon, but just before this it is possible to make an escape if needed.

The high flows of this canyon destroy the anchors rapidly, making a bolting kit essential in here. The first abseil from old piton anchors, is fairly simple but aquatic. The second however, is inescapable and this is where anchors are easily stripped away and may require pitons / bolts to be placed. This amazing aquatic abseil drops you into a deep pool below, behind the waterfall. Climb out of here and down into the larger, deeper section of the gorge. The canyon walls now grow tall and tower over as you gorge-walk through the bottom section. Near the end, the river flattens for a short while before reaching a series of waterfalls. Here you can find plenty of jumps and small slides to relax and play on before ending your journey down the canyon.

When the river flattens again just after the last waterfall, you can exit river-right to find a forest track winding its way back uphill. Follow this road all the way up to the A832 then turn right, back to your vehicle.

## Water level marker

This river has a dam situated a little further upstream of the get-in. It is best to check the flow at the first abseil. The flow here should not look too intimidating and pushy for the abseil. If it looks too strong then do not descend as the main waterfall will be far too powerful and dangerous.

No escape

# Black Rock Gorge

| Star rating | ★★★★ |
|---|---|
| Grade | 5 C/D |
| River | River Glass |
| Duration | 10mins / 30mins approach – 3 to 4hrs descent – 10mins return |
| Canyon length | 2km |
| Longest abseil | 12m (Access abseil 40m) |
| Parking A | NH 582 667 (57.6674, -4.3796) |
| Parking B | NH 597 670 (57.6708, -4.3539) |
| In | NH 581 665 ((57.6658, -4.3803) |
| Out | NH 596 668 (57.6697, -4.3551) |

## Canyon description

Black Rock Gorge is the UK's most committing canyon descent. The steep conglomer-
ate rock walls feel ever so intimidating as you descend down into its depths.
**Warning** - This narrow gorge contains many fallen trees and debris that can change
frequently, creating siphons and other hazards. This difficult descent requires you to
be adequately prepared as there are no escape routes.

**5**

## Getting there

Drive north out of Inverness on the A9 going over Kessock Bridge. Stay on the A9
heading north and you will cross over a second bridge. After this bridge, stay on the

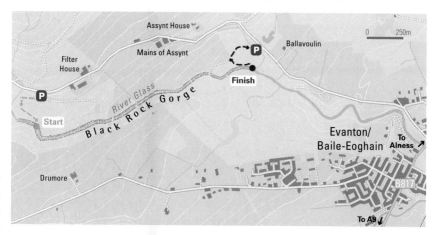

A9 for just over a mile until you see the signs for Evanton. Turn off left here towards the village of Evanton. Continue through the village and take the left turn just past the road bridge, signposted for Glenglass. There are two options to park your car:

To park at the top of the gorge (Parking A), drive for exactly 2 miles up this road and you will see a turning left into a forestry road. You'll know it's the right spot as there is no gate blocking access. Park here.

To park near the bottom (Parking B), drive up the same road but pull into a layby that has a footpath signpost for Black Rock Gorge.

## Approach

From the forestry parking spot at the top, walk down the track on your right until you reach a fence. Walk left along the overgrown forestry road that heads back towards Evanton. At the end of this fence you can see into the gorge beside a few trees. Here is where you can access the riverside. Using any solid tree as your anchor, abseil down into the gorge and begin your descent.

If you have parked at the lower parking area, follow the marked trail to Black Rock Gorge. You will cross over one of two viewing bridges giving you a good look into what's to come. Now on the river-right side, follow a trail leading up away from the gorge to the main trail path. Turn right to walk in the upstream direction. Stay straight as the path splits a few times to the left. After about 5–10mins you will reach an overgrown track, leading you down to a grey bridge and pipeline. Cross this bridge then walk along the fence to find a small gate. Pass through and continue to walk along the overgrown forest road upstream to the access point.

## Descent

Abseil down into the gorge at the end of the fence-line to start your descent. Following the river as it winds its way through narrow walls, you will come across many different features created by natural debris. At the time of writing, the larger features have been bolted to avoid the main flow. One smaller but hydraulic drop just before the grey pipeline bridge comes into sight has a hand-line bolt up to a higher bolt river-right to avoid the flow. The gorge gradually gets deeper as you approach the two viewing bridges above and there are a few tricky features to navigate in these depths.

Once you pass the last bridge the gorge walls will begin to open out a bit and the end is near. Just a couple more natural log jams to pass before you swim out of the gorge to your exit. Climb up the ladder to your left to gain the path above. Follow this back upstream towards the lower car parking spot. If parked at the top, follow approach directions from lower car parking or walk up the road.

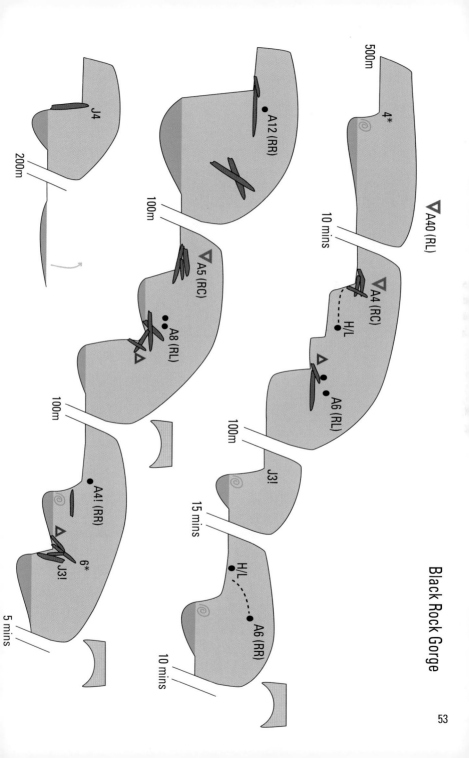

Black Rock Gorge

**5**

Water level marker

This canyoning route requires the lowest of water levels and there is a hydro scheme above that can be unpredictable. Wait for a long dry spell.

The water levels can be checked from the road bridge in the village of Evanton. Looking over the bridge into the stream you should see a calm river with plenty of rocks uncovered by water. If most of the rocks are covered then the gorge is going to be very dangerous.

The better position to check the water levels is at the top below the dam pipe over the river. You can access this location from the upper car parking spot. When you walk down the track and reach the fence as with the approach, turn right instead and follow another track down through a gate to find the pipe. The river here should be gentle and a large boulder with a patch of moss on top in the centre should have no water flowing over it or even near the top.

# Meig Gorge

| Star rating | ★ |
|---|---|
| Grade | 1 B/C |
| River | River Meig |
| Duration | 2mins approach – 1hr 30mins descent – 20mins return |
| Canyon length | 900m |
| Parking | NH 377 559 (57.5642, -4.7157) |
| In | NH 376 560 (57.5651, -4.7166) |
| Out | NH 386 564 (57.5692, -4.6995) |

## Canyon description

A beautiful display of natural rock features and lots of swimming fill this gorge-walk. Situated just below Meig Dam, it is often low enough to descend but the tight gorge does create strong flows in areas. You may encounter a kayaker or two.

## Getting there

From Muir of Ord, take the A832 to Marybank. In the centre of this village take a turning off to drive up towards Strathconon. After about 8 miles you will reach Meig Dam and can park in a layby beside the forest road. Ensure you don't block any access.

**6**

## Approach

Simply walk down the grassy slopes below the dam to access the river.

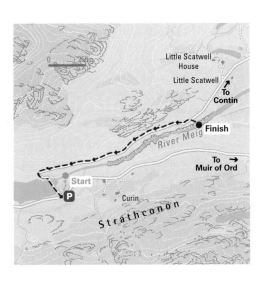

## Descent

The gorge is simple to navigate. Follow the river down past the weir and the gorge will start to get deeper. Even when the river is at its lowest, there are some strong currents to be aware of. Make your way carefully

down and around the multiple drops, discovering a few small jumps and slides as you go. One of the larger jumps can be found up a short climb, river-left, at a larger rapid that drops to the left into a deep pool. A rope may be in place to climb back up for another go. Not far past this you will discover a beautiful natural archway that you swim under.

After a little more gorge-walking, the steep sides start to shallow out and the river flattens. Look for an egress point on the river-left side. Hike up through the trees to gain the road. Now just walk back upstream on this road, cross the dam and arrive back at your vehicle.

## Water level marker

It's best to go when there hasn't been a lot of rain. Just walk along the dam to look into the river below. You only want to descend this gorge when the dam is releasing the standard compensation flow. The water flowing out the river-left side at the bottom of the dam should look very gentle. For a gorge walker this flow is more than enough, any more than this will require some strong white-water swimming. A lot more, requires a kayak.

Amazing archway

Descending the falls

# Strath-Canyon

| Star rating | ★★ |
| --- | --- |
| Grade | 4 A/B |
| River | River Taodail |
| Duration | 30mins approach – 2 to 2.5hrs descent – 10mins return |
| Canyon length | 1.4km (700m from early access point) |
| Longest abseil | 11m |
| Parking | NG 942 421 (57.4227, -5.4292) |
| Upper start | NG 958 417 (57.4197, -5.4023) |
| Lower start | NG 952 421 (57.4232, -5.4127) |
| Out | NG 946 422 (57.4236, -5.4213) |

## Canyon description

The stream is open to start before it carves its way through into a deep gorge, with the main waterfall locked inside these canyon walls. Deep pools and carved rocks make this an interesting descent.

## Getting there

Head up the A87 going towards Kyle of Lochalsh, the road to the Isle of Skye. Just a few miles before you reach Kyle of Lochalsh, take the turning right signposted for Strathcarron A890. Drive along this rollercoaster of a road until you reach

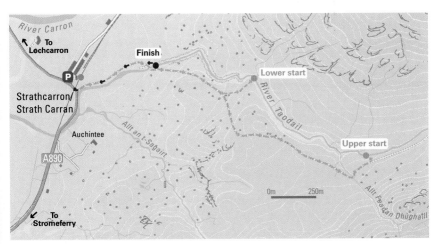

Strathcarron. Park in the car park behind the Strathcarron Hotel, in the centre of the village.

## Approach

Walk back across the railway crossing and take the immediate left turn through a sheep pen. Follow a track along the side of the river; it will cross over and head uphill on the river-left side. After roughly 20mins on the track you will cross a small stream, turn left off the road here and walk down to the river. Get in above or below the first smooth waterfall.

Lower start – If you want to skip the long gorge-walk at the top you can choose to access the canyon at the top of all the action by following alongside the river when the forest road starts to bend away. Follow the canyon side to a corner where you'll find an obvious anchor off a large tree to enter the canyon via an abseil.

## Descent

The beginning section from the top of this canyon is quite open and has a few easy features to negotiate as you gorge-walk down into the canyon walls. A local canyon-ing company uses this route and makes use of the lower access point. If you are also using this lower start, you begin your descent by abseiling off the large tree above and into the canyon in two pitches. From the bottom of the lower start, you'll find some bolts to help access the waterfall when the river is high. An aquatic abseil here or a daring toboggan from the top, but for those who abseil down you can still climb back up, river-right, to access the toboggan from a lower position.

Following this is the largest waterfall, which offers a spectacular 2-pitch abseil. The second pitch can be a little sticky when retrieving your rope. For those who dare, this waterfall has a technical jump from a ledge on the river-left side. It requires some delicate abseiling to get to it from the first pitch bolts (abseil 14m). The landing area needs inspection!

There is one more good jump off the next waterfall before the remainder of the beautiful gorge levels out and becomes another long gorge-walk. Eventually the gorge walls shallow and you can make an exit out, river-left and walk back down along the track, to the village.

## Water level marker

This is simple to check. The river flowing by the road is the outflow of the canyon. It should be flowing gently, with a large boulder beach on the river-left side. If most of this beach is covered and the river is very high, the canyon may be dangerous in parts but experienced canyoneers may still descend with care.

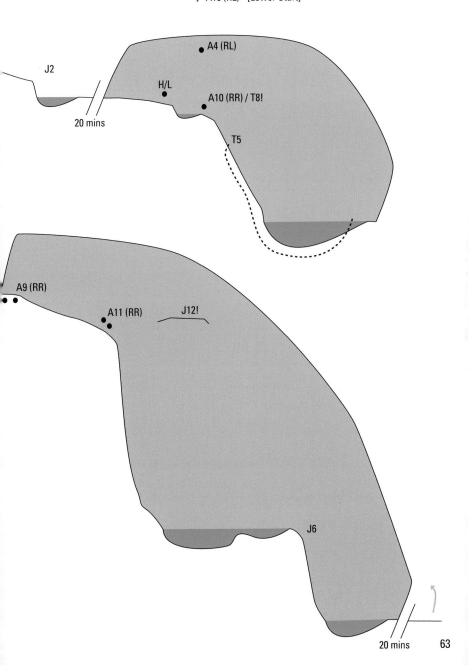

A10 (RL) - [Lower Start]

A4 (RL)

J2

H/L

A10 (RR) / T8!

20 mins

T5

A9 (RR)

A11 (RR)

J12!

J6

The main event

# Falls of Foyers

| | |
|---|---|
| **Star rating** | ★★ |
| **Grade** | 3 A |
| **River** | Foyer River |
| **Duration** | 1min approach – 2.5hrs descent – 35mins return |
| **Canyon length** | 1.3km |
| **Longest abseil** | 58m |
| **Parking** | NH 498 199 (57.2453, -4.4912) |
| **In** | NH 498 199 (57.2454, -4.4907) |
| **Out** | NH 495 209 (57.2535, -4.4962) |

## Canyon description

A fine outing down a beautiful Scottish canyon on the banks of Loch Ness. While mostly scenic gorge-walking and peaceful swims, it's interrupted by the giant waterfall in the middle.

## Getting there

Heading south from Inverness, take the B862 towards Dores and turn off right onto the B852 for Foyers. Follow this road along the side of Loch Ness and eventually the road leads up into the village of Foyers. Pass on through the village and past a playground on your left. As you pass this and begin to head out of Foyers, look for a small turning right. Turn in here and cross over a tight bridge to a small grass parking area beside the river.

Heading north from Fort Augustus, take the B862 out along the east side of Loch Ness. Drive along this road until you reach the turning left for Foyers. After a few minutes along this road, you reach the

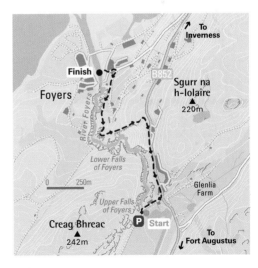

8

65

village of Foyers. Before you enter the village, take the small turning left just after the obvious dam in the river. Drive across the tight bridge to a small grass parking area.

## Approach

Easy – walk down into the river, less than a minute from the parking area.

## Descent

It starts off with a good thrill, an obvious bold jump into the deep pool below, but it is possible to clamber down the river-right side. After this comes a long gorge-walking journey through a beautiful canyon. Then, eventually, you will reach the top of the main event. The bolts are situated high up on the top of a ledge, river-right, that involves a bit of tricky climbing to get to. This is because the high volume of water that this canyon gets will strip any anchors close to the lip. If you can't climb direct to them, you can scramble up a gully on the right (just upstream) to gain a tree filled ledge above and then use a tree anchor to abseil to the bolts.

After this awesome pitch comes a boulder strewn gorge-walk down in the depths of the canyon, with a small jump tucked away near the bottom of the gorge. When you see the first bridge crossing the river, swim along just past this and exit river-right. Clamber up to the road above, (you should come out beside a bus stop).

To get back, walk up the road and turn right when you see the footpath sign for the Falls of Foyers. Follow the footpath trail back upstream past a few viewpoints and keep heading uphill; you'll reach the road at the top beside the shop. Now just walk back along the road towards where you parked the car.

## Water level marker

This river is dam controlled, and the water is taken out just before the get-in. You can easily check what's going on from where you park. Ideally you want to see a trickle of water making its way into the canyon here. Anything more than that may prove treacherous but managable for an experienced group of canyoneers. The dam takes away almost all the flow but it's best after a little dry weather.

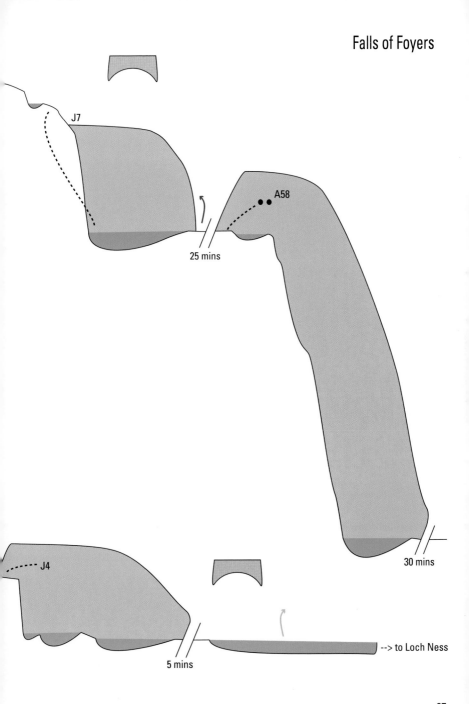

J7

A58

25 mins

30 mins

J4

5 mins

--> to Loch Ness

Andy 'sending it'

# Sligachan Gorge

| Star rating | ★ |
|---|---|
| Grade | 3 A/B |
| River | Allt Daraich |
| Duration | 15mins approach – 1hr descent – 5mins return |
| Canyon length | 700m |
| Longest abseil | 11m |
| Parking | NG 488 299 (57.2904, -6.1711) |
| In | NG 493 294 (57.2865, -6.1620) |
| Out | NG 488 296 (57.2882, -6.1698) |

## Canyon description

This small, beautiful gorge sits right next to the lovely Sligachan Hotel, overlooked by the Cuillin mountains. Crystal clear waters and interesting little features makes this a fantastic hidden alternative to the popular 'Fairy Pools' of Skye.

## Getting there

9

As you cross the bridge onto the Isle of Skye at Kyle of Lochalsh, keep heading north on the A87. After about 30 minutes of driving, you will reach Sligachan. There is a parking area on your left before you reach the hotel. Park here.

## Approach

From the car park, begin walking along the trail that leads up to the monument. Take the left-hand track along the side of the gorge and go through the metal gate where the path splits. Follow the trail uphill and eventually it will split again. Stay left and this will lead you to the start of the gorge where the river is flat. Get in just above a small slot.

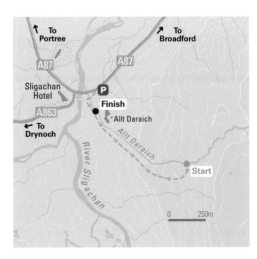

Tranquillity

## Descent

The route begins with an optional bridging downclimb through the flow, a good way to immerse yourself in that fresh water. Small waterfalls lead down to a short abseil. The next larger feature is a good jump off the ledge, river-right or if the water-levels are good, there is a technical slide that you can climb down to; but lean left! Afterwards is a nice but long gorge-walk through broken boulders.

Near the end of this gorge is a lovely final jump off the river-right side. Just a little further downstream look for an obvious exit river-left, following a track uphill that brings you out beside the metal gate near the start. Now just follow the path back to the car park, or to the Sligachan restaurant for good food.

## Water level marker

From the car park, walk down a path that leads towards the River Sligachan. Before you reach the bigger river, you walk onto a small bridge over the Allt Daraich. Here you can check the flow. This gorge could be descended in higher flows but ideally you don't want to see the rocks completely covered in the river here at the bridge.

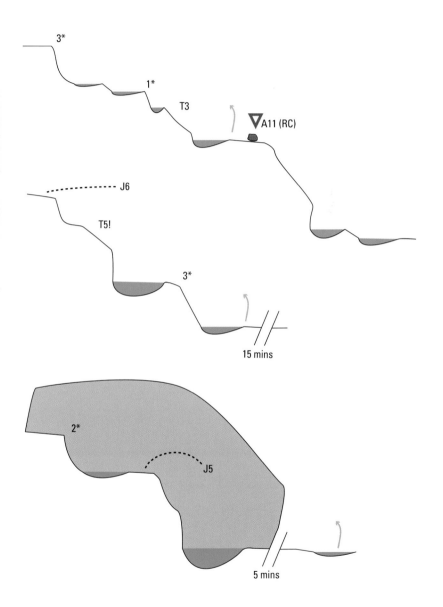

Andy on the 2nd drop

# Lealt Falls

| | |
|---|---|
| **Star rating** | ★★ |
| **Grade** | 3 B/C |
| **River** | Lealt River |
| **Duration** | 5mins approach – 1hr descent – 15mins return |
| **Canyon length** | 450m |
| **Longest abseil** | 36m |
| **Parking** | NG 518 605 (57.5663, -6.1517) |
| **In** | NG 515 604 (57.5651, -6.1569) |
| **Out** | NG 519 604 (57.5652, -6.1508) |

## Canyon description

While only a short canyoning trip, these three waterfalls offer up an epic descent on Skye, finishing down by the sea. And you can park right beside them!

## Getting there

Head north out of Portree on the A855, up the east coastline. Drive along this road for about 12 miles, passing by the Old Man of Storr. As you approach Lealt and cross over the road bridge, you will see a large coach parking area on your right. Pull into here and drive through to the main car park above it. Park here.

**10**

## Approach

Walk back down through the coach park and back along the road to the road bridge over the river. Climb over a fence on the upstream side of the bridge, river-left. Easily walk down a grass slope to the Lealt River.

## Descent

Walk under the road bridge and approach the first abseil

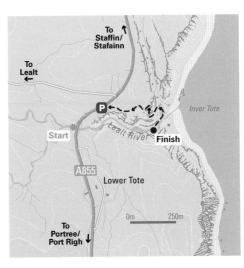

The big finale

on the river-left side. The waterfall below has a cool walk behind once you are down. The next waterfall offers up an aquatic pitch down the river-right side into a deep pool below. To reach the anchor may require a little climb. After this abseil, a long gorge walk leads you down to the big finale – a large cascade into a deep pool below. You will need to scramble up on the river-right side and traverse along to a strong tree anchor that offers a fantastic abseil, often with an audience watching from afar. Once you're down and have taken it all in, begin walking along river-left and up the obvious steep track back to the car park.

This route is due to be bolted sometime in 2021 as follows: The 2nd waterfall will have two pitches bolted river-left. The final pitch will have handline bolts to an anchor, river-right.

### Water level marker

As this is a larger river than most canyons, it will often have a fair amount of flow, but each abseil is placed to avoid the majority of the danger. You can easily check the river from the newly built viewing platform. If the top of the first waterfall looks as if it would be dangerous to wade across – do not descend!

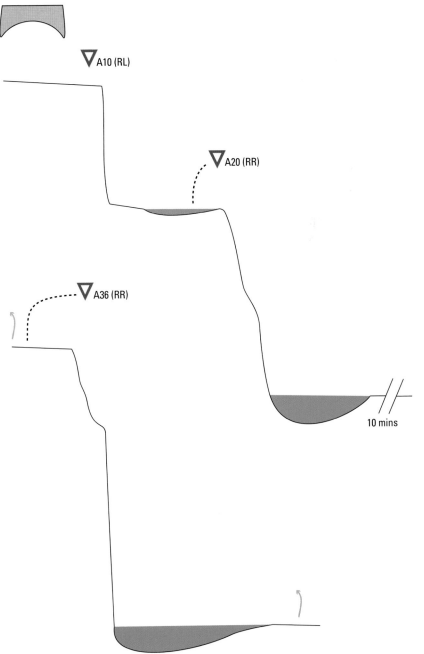

A10 (RL)

A20 (RR)

A36 (RR)

10 mins

Surprising slot section

# Ben More Canyon

| Star rating | ★★ |
|---|---|
| Grade | 4 A/B |
| River | Abhainn na h-Uamha |
| Duration | 20mins approach – 1hr 30mins descent – 3min return |
| Canyon length | 900m |
| Longest abseil | 12m |
| Parking | NM 507 368 (56.4569, -6.0481) |
| In | NM 514 360 (56.4505, -6.0352) |
| Out | NM 508 367 (56.4564, -6.0462) |

## Canyon description

An unexpected canyon route down two hidden slot sections at the foot of Ben More. Adventurous with some daring jumps into crystal clear waters, nestled amongst great scenery on the Isle of Mull.

## Getting there

Take either the Oban ferry or Lochaline ferry over to the Isle of Mull. When you arrive, head north on the A849 to Salen. At Salen, take a left turn along the B8035 and stay on this road through Gruline. When the road heads along the side of Loch Na Keal, drive for no more than 2.5 miles and you will reach the bridge that passes over the canyon end. Park off the road by the bridge.

## Approach

From the layby, begin walking towards the new pumphouse and follow the trail that heads up the river-right side of the river towards Ben More. Simply keep walking up this track until you can see you are above the first of the two slot sections. Get in above

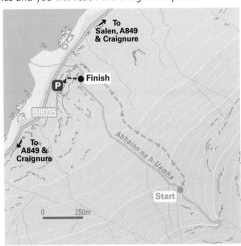

11

77

📷 Crystal-clear waters

some small drops that are upstream of a sharp turn in the river. Easily access the river above these drops.

## Descent

**11**

A fun start to this route with a small refreshing jump, a little slide and then another small but rather shallow jump. A bit of downclimbing and a short gorge-walk brings you along to the two main drops in the upper slot section. Bolts on the river-right side drop you easily to the next larger waterfall. As of March 2021, bolts at the next waterfall have been damaged by high water but remain usable with extreme caution (they will be replaced in the future). If you don't fancy abseiling, take on the daring jump but be sure to get some distance.

Following this is some beautiful gorge-walking with one awkward drop at a broken pipe. When the slot ends, you can cut across the heather to the start of the next slot section.

The beginning of this section starts with either an abseil or a daring tight jump from up on the river-right side. Now just cruise your way down the gorge to the finish. Simply walk back down to the road and your vehicle.

## Water level marker

The water level is simple to view from the road bridge at the bottom. Ideally you want to see a gentle flow of water in the stream. Anything more than normal flow after a few dry days may be a bit pushy but still accessible for the more experienced canyoneer.

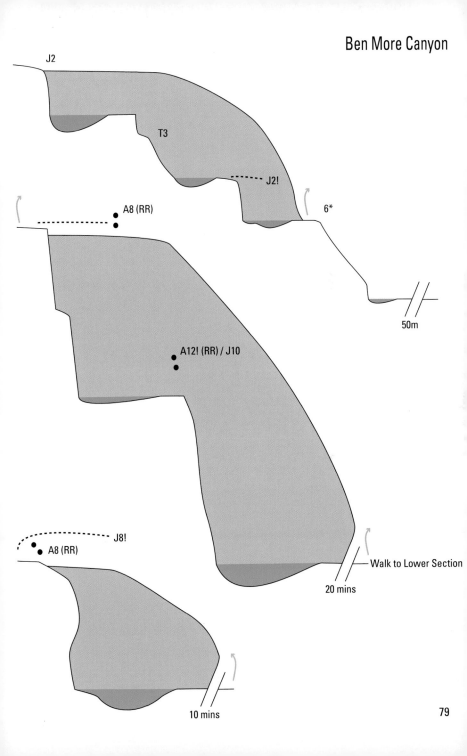

# Ben More Canyon

J2

T3

J2!

A8 (RR)

6*

50m

A12! (RR) / J10

J8!

A8 (RR)

Walk to Lower Section

20 mins

10 mins

# West Coast

West is Best! That's the saying amongst those who live on the dramatic west coast of Scotland, where the mountains are big and fortunately the canyons are too. The steeper terrain and constant rain here provides the perfect breeding ground for canyons, giving you lots of options to choose from.

Down to the sea

Django checking if it goes

# Sax Canyon

| | |
|---|---|
| **Star rating** | ★★★ |
| **Grade** | 4+ B/C |
| **River** | Allt a' Choire Reidh |
| **Duration** | 50mins approach – 3 to 4hrs descent – 40mins return |
| **Canyon length** | 800m |
| **Longest abseil** | 35m |
| **Parking** | NG 953 065 (57.1039, -5.3813) |
| **In** | NG 937 082 (57.1185, -5.4095) |
| **Out** | NG 935 078 (57.1140, -5.4129) |

## Canyon description

A stunning canyon located by a sea-loch in the remote, far west of Scotland. You'll find beautiful waterfalls carving their way down the hillside followed by a long swim in the sea to make your return. An adventurous day out.

## Getting there

You need to drive to the very remote village of Kinloch Hourn. Head to Invergarry on the A82 south of Inverness. Take the turning west on the A87 – Road to the Isles. About 5 miles up this road there is a turning left, off the main road, signposted for

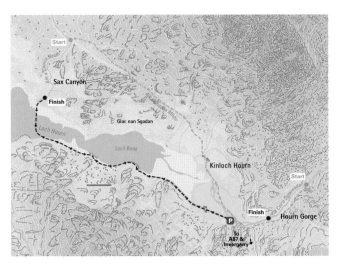

**12**

Kinloch Hourn. Follow this long road to the very end by the village. As you reach the village, park in the only car park on the right.

## Approach

Start walking over the estuary to the north-side and gain the main track that leads past a house and up the hillside. Follow this path upwards and west. You should be following a line of pylons over the hillside. The path will drop back down over the hill and meet the river that flows to the canyon. Get in here.

## Descent

The journey begins with a shallow river walk for a little while before the first small toboggan followed by a larger waterfall. Some more gorge-walking after this abseil brings you to the main part of the canyon. Here the first, sloped waterfall can be jumped by walking up and out along the river-right side to a good ledge. Check the pool. The canyon steepens and a variety of wonderful waterfalls descend down the hillside. Anchors may need rigging.

The final steep waterfall drops into a shallow gorge below and eventually the river flattens bringing you to an old footbridge. The easiest way back now is to swim over 200m across Loch Hourn to a good path that will lead you back to the car. Don't forget to wash your kit after the salt-water swim!

**12**

## Water level marker

The only way to tell beforehand is by hiking for about 20mins around the south side of Loch Hourn so that you can see the river. If it doesn't look like a huge torrent of white water then it is good to go. Otherwise, you can gauge it just before you get in. The river at the top should be flowing gently down for the canyon to be a good level. Most abseils avoid the flow and can be descended in higher flows with caution.

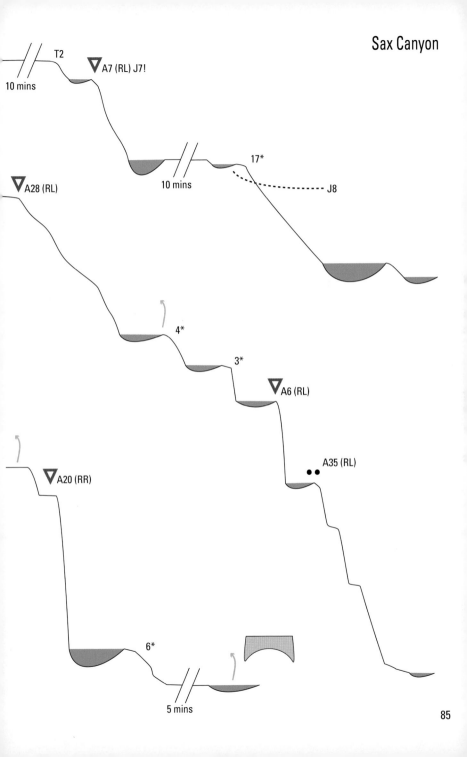

Mini gorge

# Hourn Gorge

| Star rating | ★ |
|---|---|
| Grade | 3 A/B |
| River | Allt Coire Sgoireadail |
| Duration | 40mins approach – 2hrs descent – 10mins return |
| Canyon length | 450m |
| Longest abseil | 18m |
| Parking | NG 953 065 (57.1039, -5.3813) |
| In | NG 960 068 (57.1063, -5.3707) |
| Out | NG 957 065 (57.1039, -5.3748) |

## Canyon description

A wild gorge on the far west coast of Scotland. Full of abseils and fun features, it makes a great companion gorge to the Sax Canyon. While not as impressive, it is worth doing after driving so far.

## Getting there

Follow the same directions as for Sax Canyon. Park in the only car park by a right-hand turn.

**13**

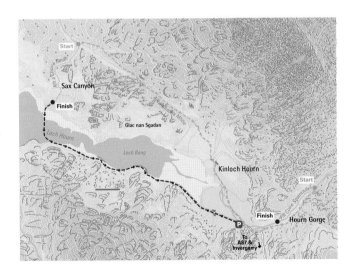

## Approach

Start walking back up the road out of Kinloch Hourn. At a right-hand bend, turn off the road over a slab of rock in the river and begin trekking uphill. You should be walking up the river-left side of the gorge. There is no path so it's easiest to follow the fence line. Get in where the river starts to flatten out above some old dam structures.

## Descent

This canyon has only been descended by a few people, so anchors may need to be built. The gorge starts off quite steep with most of the abseils near the start. There is quite the variety of waterfalls in this canyon which make it fun for rigging, but nothing too complicated. A few shallow jumps and bumpy toboggans are to be discovered too. After a double-pool drop abseil, the gorge begins to ease off and becomes a boulder strewn riverbed.

When the river flattens out you can exit river-left and continue walking alongside the stream until you can make your way back up to the road. Then stroll back down to the car park area.

**13**

## Water level marker

The water level can be checked from the car park. The river flowing into the village should look like a gentle stream. Most rocks should be uncovered. If the river here is flowing strongly the gorge may be very treacherous. No information is available for high water descent.

Steve admiring the arch

# Butterfly Burn

| Star rating | ★★★ |
| --- | --- |
| Grade | 3 B |
| River | Allt Mhuic |
| Duration | 20mins approach - 1hr 30mins descent |
| Canyon length | 500m |
| Longest abseil | 12m |
| Parking | NN 120 911 (56.9732, -5.0941) |
| In | NN 123 917 (56.9786, -5.0907) |
| Out | NN 120 912 (56.9740, -5.0946) |

## Canyon description

A great wee canyon with lots of deep pools, and easy to escape. There are plenty of jumps, some slides and good abseils. A brilliant canyon for all, especially if you are starting out canyoning.
**Please note that this canyon sits within a butterfly reserve**. Please keep to the paths when not in the riverbed and leave no trace.

14

## Getting there

Following the directions for Antler Canyon (Route 16), continue past this for another 5 miles along the Loch Arkaig road. You will eventually reach a small forestry car park on your right, just before a wooden bridge. Park here. You should find a forestry information sign about the butterfly reserve beside the car park.

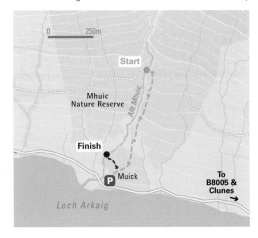

## Approach

One of the easiest approaches to a canyon. Go through the gate and follow the grass path straight uphill until you reach a forest road going over the burn. Get in above the first feature upstream of the bridge.

📷 Technical jump!

## 14

### Descent

Descending the first few features you will find bolts just below the bridge river-right. These are for use in higher flows and for training. The canyon ahead has plenty of pools to plunge into and check out. One bumpy toboggan too. The first abseil of the two-tier falls has an anchor but can be jumped after inspection of the tight landing area. Bolts for the second tier are low down on the right.

Now the gorge sides start to get a bit steeper as you head along to the final abseil. A tree on the right gives the best line to abseil down but bolts are also available on the left for a more aquatic option.

Head under a beautiful natural arch and carry on downstream to an obvious exit left. Walk up and over the grass bank and you'll meet the path back to the car.

### Water level marker

This canyon generally has low flows and will look like a trickle in the burn by the car park. If the burn is running fast, the canyon is high but may still be suitable for experienced canyoneers. It is a good option if everything else is too high.

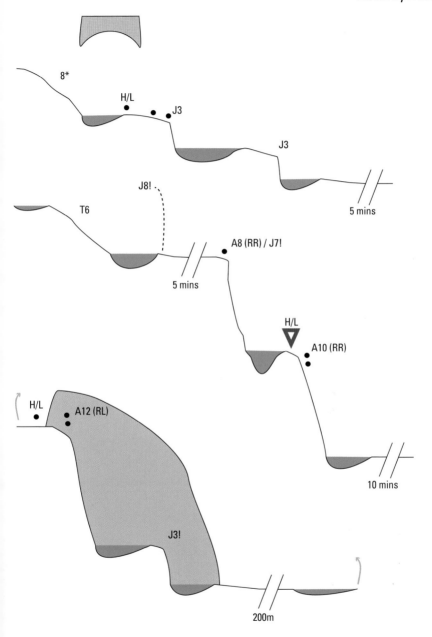

Deep upper section

# Chia-aig Falls

| | |
|---|---|
| **Star rating** | ★★ |
| **Grade** | 4+ B/C |
| **River** | Abhainn Chia-aig |
| **Duration** | 45mins approach – 4hrs descent |
| **Canyon length** | 1.9km |
| **Longest abseil** | 18m |
| **Parking** | NN 176 889 (56.9548, -5.0009) |
| **In** | NN 181 904 (56.9694, -4.9938) |
| **Out** | NN 176 889 (56.9550, -5.0012) |

## Canyon description

One of the longest canyons in the Scottish Highlands and a brilliant one to descend. Full of slides, jumps, abseils and plenty of gorge-walking through steep and impressive canyon walls.

## Getting there

Follow the directions for Antler Canyon (Route 16), then continue along the road for just a few hundred metres past Antler to reach a large carpark and a layby by an old stone bridge. Park here.

## Approach

Start heading up the path beside the waterfalls, heading through a large gate and up to a gravel forest road. Keep following the road that goes uphill and along into the glen with the river to your left. When

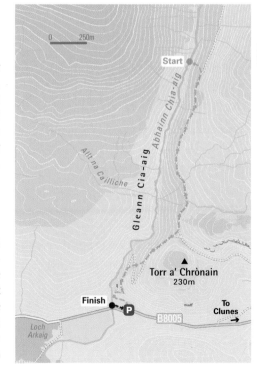

you can see the river begin to flatten out to a gentle riverbed you will be able to descend towards the river down a gravel track before breaking off and climbing over a deer fence. It is possible to access the canyon earlier along the road if you'd like to make it shorter or avoid the first two complicated abseils.

## Descent

At the beginning of your descent there are two abseils, the second of which can be dangerous in anything other than low water. This abseil is tight and the waterfall can be pushy as you drop into a concealed cauldron. In here it can be difficult to escape when there is a lot of flow because the exit channel is small and you are behind the flow. Once you are past these abseils you will be rewarded with tall carved rock walls before it opens out. The remainder of the canyon is a lot less complicated and you will discover some cool jumps, bumpy toboggans, and lots of gorge-walking through an inescapable passage.

Take care in this canyon as there are lots of shallow pools and hidden boulders underwater that may catch you out and the majority of this route is very hard to escape. The largest jump of 10m may prove difficult to rig as an abseil but it is possible to exit river-left just before and walk around if you choose to. The pool below the jump has an underwater ledge and requires a large leap. After this jump it is possible to exit river-left back up to the forest road before you commit yourself with an abseil into the remainder of the twisting canyon.

Eventually the route will open out again beside the hydro-scheme pump house. Just past this, there is an abseil off an old fence post river-left and then you reach the final two waterfalls. The last pool has become shallower over time and may no longer be deep enough to jump. Exit easily river-left to the car park.

## Water level marker

This canyon has a large catchment area so be warned if going in on a rainy day. Even with the new hydro scheme above the canyon, the water can rise rapidly. You can easily check the flow from the final two waterfalls by the road. The last waterfall should look like a curtain of water that you can easily see through. If it's a thicker curtain of water, the upper section will be too dangerous. If the two waterfalls are solid white water, do not descend!

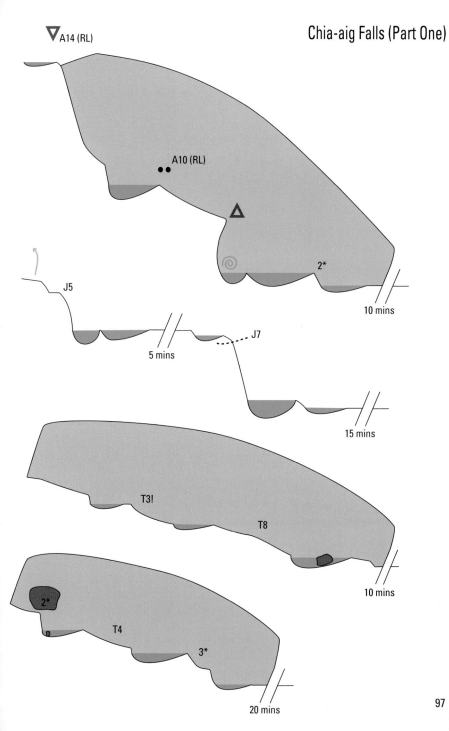

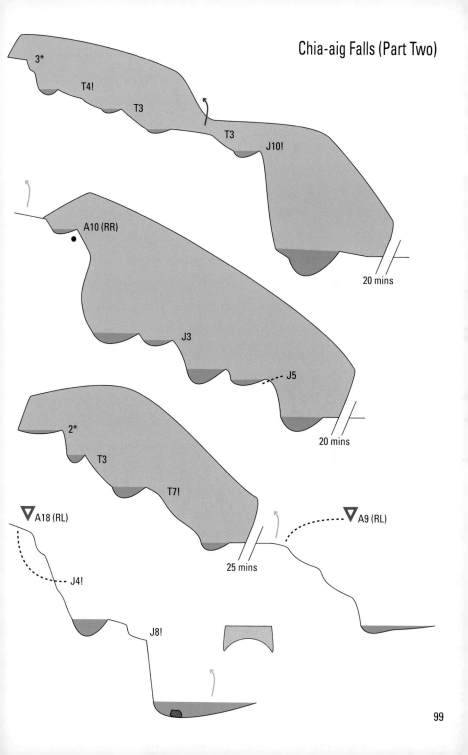

3*

T4!

T3

T3

J10!

A10 (RR)

20 mins

J3

J5

20 mins

2*

T3

T7!

▽ A18 (RL)

▽ A9 (RL)

25 mins

J4!

J8!

Matt in the flow

Downclimbing ski

# Antler Canyon

| | |
|---|---|
| **Star rating** | ★★★ |
| **Grade** | 4 B |
| **River** | Allt Bhan |
| **Duration** | 1hr approach – 3 to 4hrs descent |
| **Canyon length** | 750m |
| **Longest abseil** | 55m |
| **Parking** | NN 197 888 (56.9550, -4.9670) |
| **In** | NN 198 895 (56.9617, -4.9652) |
| **Out** | NN 197 888 (56.9553, -4.9665) |

## Canyon description

An incredibly steep canyon tucked away not far from Fort William, offering spectacular views of Ben Nevis. It consists mainly of abseils with a few jumps and slides. There
are plenty of natural anchors along the way.

## Getting there

16

Drive north out of Spean Bridge on the A82 and take the left-hand turn at the
Commando Memorial. Follow the road past the memorial and down towards Gairlochy.
Once you reach this small village, continue along the road over the canal and take a
right, following signs for Loch Arkaig. Follow this road for about 4 miles and you will
reach a few houses where
the road bends to the left.
A few hundred metres past
this bend you will cross a
small bridge, park off the
road immediately after this
bridge.

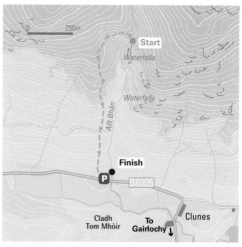

## Approach

The route up to the can-
yon's start is a beast! Head
straight up through the
trees on river-right and
just keep going. Do not try

Winter canyoning

**16**

to follow the contours or attempt to keep the river in view as it will get too steep and dangerous. Eventually you will make it out of the woods but keep going up the hill. As the gradient starts to level off, the first twisting waterfall should come into view. You can either get in above or below this waterfall.

## Descent

The majority of the abseils in this canyon already have some form of existing anchor in place; however these can often be destroyed by the river over time. If you choose to tackle the first large waterfall you may find it difficult to rig the abseil. Further downstream there is a small toboggan above a bigger waterfall abseil – you will need to rig this abseil before you slide in as it is hard to reach any anchors from the pool. After this waterfall comes a monster of a pitch, the long slanting 55m waterfall. The walls start to close in as you gorge-walk along to the final few abseils / downclimbs, eventually making your way out of the gorge. The road is straight ahead.

## Water level marker

The burn next to where you park is the canyon, although it won't look like much. Usually there will be a small amount of water coming down the stream. If it has quite a lot of water, the canyon is going to be too dangerous to descend.

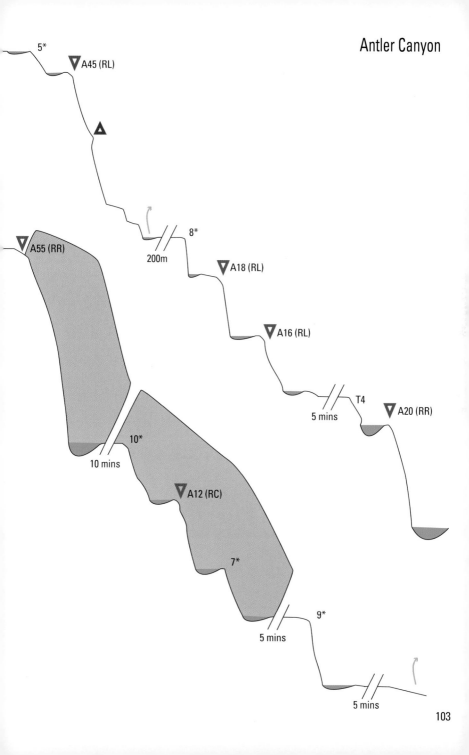

Antler Canyon

5*

A45 (RL)

A55 (RR)

8*

200m

A18 (RL)

A16 (RL)

T4

5 mins

A20 (RR)

10*

10 mins

A12 (RC)

7*

9*

5 mins

5 mins

Steve showing his skills
– The Adventure Photograph

# Laggan Canyon

| Star rating | ★★ |
| --- | --- |
| Grade | 3 B/C |
| River | Allt Na h-Uamha |
| Duration | 20mins approach – 1 to 2hrs descent – 5mins return |
| Canyon length | 450m |
| Longest abseil | 20m |
| Parking | NN 401 819 (56.9006, -4.6274) |
| In | NN 400 822 (56.9035, -4.6288) |
| Out | NN 400 819 (56.9004, -4.6284) |

## Canyon description

Toboggans, toboggans and more toboggans. This canyon has some wicked features for the tobogganist in you. The whole river is accessible, and escape is possible before and after each abseil. Great fun and used by canyoning companies.

## Getting there

Not too far from Spean Bridge, drive along the A86 towards Laggan. When you reach the Laggan Dam, continue along for just 2 more miles. The final waterfall can be glimpsed from the road as you cross the bridge going over it. There is a large gravel layby on the right to park in.

## Approach

Cross the road and start walking up the river-left side of the river over the stile. The trail splits in a few places but just keep heading uphill, don't take any track towards the river yet. Easier boggy walking near the top will eventually bring you back towards the river where it starts to level out. Get in by sliding down a slab.

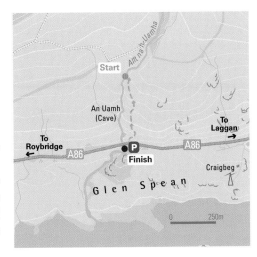

17

The big slide

**17**

## Descent

Some small shallow slides start off the canyon trip before you reach a curvy slide dropping into a deep pool. Around the corner here is the longest toboggan of the canyon. With a good flow you can toboggan about 10m. You'll most likely want to do this again, so climb back up the river-right side. A tarp sits on the left for fast slides, used by canyoning companies.

Watch out on the next toboggan; in high flows it could wash you over the next abseil. The abseil from bolt anchors drops you down behind the fall. Climb down into the pool from here. Interesting gorge-walking follows this with small slides and drops until you eventually reach the final fall. The abseil itself avoids the flow altogether. Anchors river-right. Once you've descended the last fall, continue below the road bridge around the corner to reach an area where you can climb out river-left, back up to your vehicle.

## Water level marker

You can look down to the river and the last waterfall from the road bridge. If the river below looks as if you can wade across without a problem, the canyon is at a good flow. If it looks pushy or the waterfall looks powerful, the canyon may be too dangerous to descend.

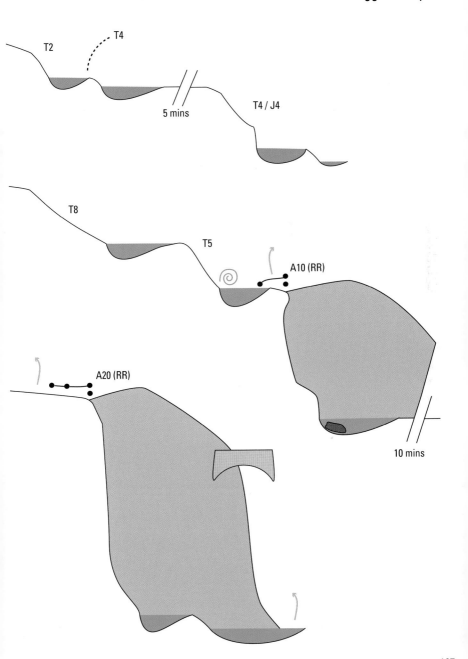

The main event

Carved gorge at the start

# Monessie Gorge

| Star rating | ★★ |
| --- | --- |
| Grade | 2 A/B |
| River | River Spean |
| Duration | 15mins approach – 1hr 30mins descent – 20mins return |
| Canyon length | 850m |
| Longest abseil | 15m |
| Parking | NN 303 809 (56.8886, -4.7878) |
| In | NN 299 810 (56.8889, -4.7930) |
| Out | NN 295 806 (56.8854, -4.8002) |

## Canyon description

One of the best easy gorge-walks in the area. Beautifully carved rocks, deep pools, and plenty of swimming. There is one epic jump in the middle for those feeling brave, or abseil if you prefer.

## Getting there

Drive east out of Spean Bridge on the A86 to Newtonmore. Once you pass through Roy Bridge drive on for no more than 2 miles. Look out for a large blue sign on the right reading 'Aite Cruinnichidh'. Once you pass this, continue along around a couple of corners. Just past a private driveway, you will see a layby on the right just ahead of you. Park here.

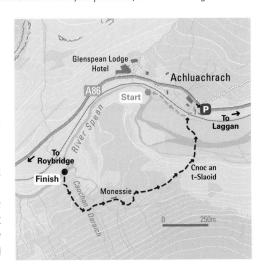

## Approach

Start walking down the track from the layby, beside the road in the direction of Roy Bridge. Head back towards the driveways you passed when you drove here. Turn left down past these houses and follow the left track down the hill and around the properties. The track will bend around to the right and over a railway crossing. Turn right after the crossing and walk along to the suspension bridge at the start of the gorge for a good view into the tight gorge at the start. To gain access, just before the bridge you can walk over the fallen fence to the riverside.

## Descent

Walk along to the first waterfall and climb down river-right. In the steep slot below this you may find some log jams that may be dangerous to manoeuvre past in higher flows, but they can be avoided by climbing around high on the right. Once out of the steep slot you will have a lovely long swim and some clambering as you navigate down the river beside the railway line above.

When you finally reach the big waterfall of about 8m you may find a perfect take-off point in the centre of the waterfall. It is possible to abseil down from a tree river-right, to a lower position for a jump or abseil all the way. After this you will navigate down through a large boulder garden filled with little caves.

Eventually the river will flatten by an old outflow. Exit river-left to a field and cross this straight ahead until you reach a track. Turn left and follow this track back to a farmhouse. Follow a path around the house and along a fence line, this route will head downhill back to the River Spean upstream of the gorge. Cross the river and walk across another field straight to the railway crossing, follow the road back to the car.

## Water level marker

You can check the flow in this gorge at the suspension bridge right at the start. The waterfall flowing in should look safe to swim around at its base. The gorge below it should be fairly still and not flowing strongly. If the base of the fall looks white and hydraulic the level is high and the gorge will be dangerous in the boulder garden because of the large number of siphons created.

© Andrew on the ropes

# Ben Nevis Gorge

| Star rating | ★★ |
|---|---|
| Grade | 3 A |
| River | Allt a Mhuilin |
| Duration | 45mins approach – 2 to 3hrs descent – 15min return |
| Canyon length | 850m |
| Longest abseil | 16m |
| Parking | NN 145 764 (56.8420, -5.0429) |
| In | NN 147 753 (56.8319, -5.0393) |
| Out | NN 140 756 (56.8351, -5.0503) |

## Canyon description

A great wee canyon with lots of easy and fun features. The majority of abseils are bolted where needed. This is another brilliant canyon for the beginner or just a good day out playing in the water that flows from the North Face of Ben Nevis.

## Getting there

Drive north out of Fort William on the A82 to Torlundy. Turn right into Torlundy and drive over the railway bridge with traffic lights. Take the right turn straight after the bridge and this gravel road will lead to the North Face car park.

**19**

## Approach

From the car park head up the trail towards the CIC hut, signposted Allt Mhuillin and viewpoint. Keep following the steep trail until you reach a bench overlooking Fort William. You can bypass a number of features by following a faint track down from here and across heather to the first steep drop. Otherwise carry on

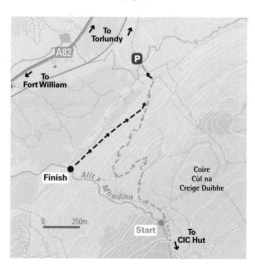

upstream for another 10mins and start crossing over the heather to the river when you reach the next picnic bench.

## Descent

If you chose to walk the extra bit, then your efforts paid off as there are a few good slides to enjoy and an unprotected drop to contend with. The first bolted feature, a steep 5m abseil into a series of pools is the start. Now you are in the main gorge. There are lots of features ahead to be enjoyed, some of which you can climb down or around. With a bit of exploration, you will find plenty of slides and small jumps. Bolts are in place for most points that may require abseiling. The last two waterfalls before the footbridge at the end aren't bolted but can be rigged for abseil.

Under the bridge, the pool below can be jumped into but changes regularly, so check first. Climb out river-left, back up to the footbridge, cross this and walk down the trail to the right of the river back down towards the car park.

## Water level marker

This canyon has a dam upstream which takes nearly all the water away from it. This makes it a brilliant option when all other canyons are too high but be warned that the dam can back up and overflow in very heavy rainfall. You can check the flow long before you reach the canyon by looking over the bridge beside the Ben Nevis Distillery. If the river looks still then it's normal, if it's flowing fast then it is too high.

**19**

Final jump

Snow and ice filled gulley

# Five Finger Gully

| Star rating | ★★ |
|---|---|
| Grade | 4+ A |
| River | Allt Coire Ghaimhnean |
| Duration | 1hr 30mins approach – 3 to 4hrs descent – 30mins return |
| Canyon length | 750m |
| Longest abseil | 50m |
| Parking | NN 123 730 (56.8108, -5.0766) |
| In | NN 150 709 (56.7926, -5.0307) |
| Out | NN 143 707 (56.7901, -5.0441) |

## Canyon description

The famous Five Finger Gully is an elusive classic amongst ice-climbers but very few canyon down it during the summer months. It is one of the more dangerous canyons with a tricky approach and loose rock overhead in the canyon. On the plus side, spectacular abseils reward your efforts as you descend off the side of Ben Nevis.

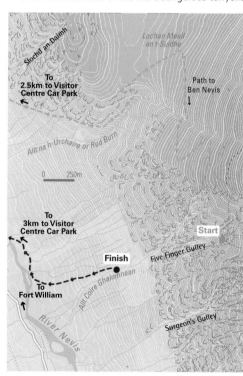

**20**

## Getting there

From Fort William, drive up the Glen Nevis road to the Ben Nevis Visitor Centre and park in the car park here.

## Approach

From the car park, cross over the footbridge and walk up towards Ben Nevis Inn (highly recommend food here). Follow the main path to the summit of

Ben Nevis. When you finally reach Lochan Meall an t-Suidhe (the halfway lochan), continue on up the zigzag path ahead. You will cross a stream that flows over the path, then up to the first turn of the zigzags. At the third turn you need to break off the path to the right, looking towards Glen Nevis. Now the dangerous approach diagonally down through loose scree begins. Take your time as you head around the contours and down to the main canyon. A large waterfall starts the canyon off, nearer to the left side of the scree gully.

## Descent

Previously made anchors in this canyon are easily stripped out during snowmelt so come prepared. The route starts off with a simple abseil at the first waterfall that plunges into the canyon, committing you to the descent. A small abseil after this does have a bolt but it's rather old now. A longer abseil follows this and then you begin to navigate your way down through Five Finger's rocky gully.

There are many more waterfalls to overcome than the topo shows, but the majority of these can be downclimbed or easily rigged for abseil if required. The gully walls open out slightly as you reach a waterfall dropping to the left. Not long after this feature, a few more low-angled waterfalls bring you to the largest and most spectacular waterfall of the canyon – a splendidly smooth 50m pitch. But it's not over, a few more abseils down into a final slot section finishes off the canyon route.

After this, you can make an exit out of the river and walk down the side to the River Nevis. Now just follow a faint track downstream along the side of the River Nevis until you meet the riverside path. Keep on this back to the footbridge and car park.

**20**

## Water level marker

The best way to inspect this river is to drive a little further up the Glen Nevis road until you can get a glimpse into the canyon. Stop in a layby where you take a good look at the main waterfall towards the bottom of the canyon. A small streak of white is ideal, you do not want much flow in here. It is ideal after a long dry spell. If the waterfall looks substantial, it is probably too high.

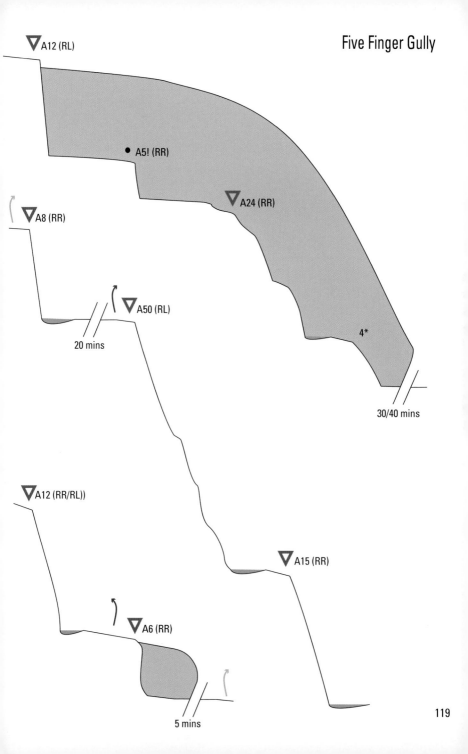

Five Finger Gully

119

Long sliding abseil

# Inchree Falls

| Star rating | ★★★ |
| --- | --- |
| Grade | 3 B/C |
| River | Abhainn Righ |
| Duration | 20mins approach – 1/1.5hr descent – 10mins return |
| Canyon length | 400m |
| Longest abseil | 35m (optional) |
| Parking | NN 030 634 (56.7206, -5.2215) |
| In | NN 032 628 (56.7150, -5.2176) |
| Out | NN 030 630 (56.7167, -5.2204) |

## Canyon description

This canyon might not be exceptionally long but it has some brilliant features that can be done again and again, making it a great canyon to play in. It's not overly committing and it's possible to walk around most features, which makes it a great venue to start out in. You will often find guided groups in here; please be respectful of their business.

## Getting there

Drive 8 miles south of Fort William on the A82. About 500m past the Corran ferry port take a turning left signposted for Inchree. The turning is just before a newly built footbridge. Follow this road as it bends around to the right, past the houses and down along to Vertical Descents. Take a right again for the forestry car park.

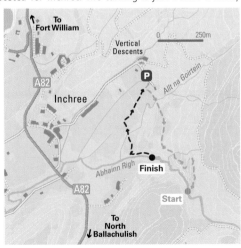

## Approach

From the forestry car park at Inchree Falls, you will need to follow a path marked waterfall walk. It's the path leading out towards the meadow, not into the woods! Just keep following this footpath, passing two good viewpoints, until you reach a bench near the top with fantastic views. An obvious boggy track leads you down towards the top of the canyon.

## Descent

Inchree Falls can be descended via different routes, both river-left or right. Bolts are dotted about for a variety of abseil choices as training courses are often run here. You will also find wires in place for the safety of commercial groups, feel free to use these if you need to but leave in place. The main falls can be abseiled river-left or avoided by climbing down beside the wire, river-right. At the base of this large waterfall is a brilliant toboggan of a few metres. In low flows this can be tobogganed from higher up, with caution. At the waterfall with the zipline, bolts offer a simple abseil river-right or a daring technical jump. Beware of underwater ledges to the right. For some added adventure, you can scramble around and behind this waterfall to some smaller jumps river-left.

The final big jump can be found not far downstream of this zipline, taking an obvious track up to a take-off area river-left. Be cautious in a small corridor downstream of this jump when the river level is high. When you reach the final pool, exit river-right and follow the obvious track along the river, taking a right through the woods and a left over an old stone wall. Keep following the path through a small stream to the field. Turn right again at a T-junction, heading back towards the car park.

## Water level marker

As you reach the first viewpoint look to the top of the longest waterfall. There is a small split stream river-right at the top. If there isn't then it's very low. If this stream is quite white, then it's high. If it's one huge brown wave, don't go in!

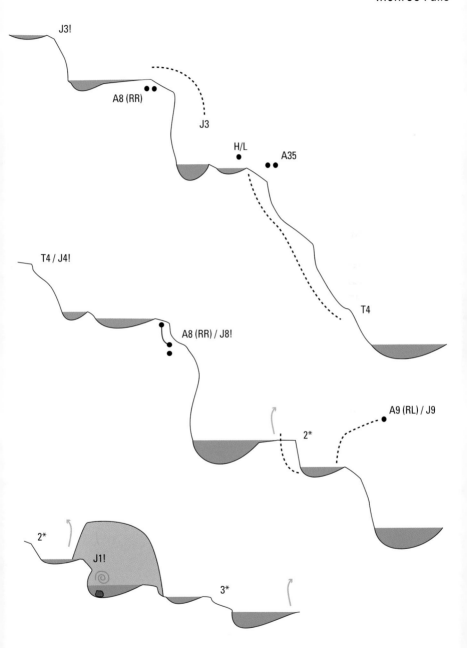

Second pitch of the Tributary

# Nathrach Tributary

| Star rating | ★ |
| --- | --- |
| Grade | 2/4 B |
| River | Allt Coire na h-Eirghe |
| Duration | 45mins approach – 40mins to 1hr descent – return via Nathrach |
| Canyon length | 450m |
| Longest abseil | 19m |
| Parking | NN 175 623 (56.7168, -4.9831) |
| In | NN 169 631 (56.7236, -4.9944) |
| Out | NN 168 629 (56.7215, -4.9955) |

## Canyon description

A brilliant partner canyon to the Nathrach (Route 23). Not the greatest trip on its own but a good start to a full day out canyoning. Interesting abseils and some good jumps, in an open but steep river, before heading over to the hill into the Allt Nathrach.

## Getting there

22

Less than a mile out of Kinlochleven on the northern road there is a quick turn right up to a small car park (4 – 5 cars). Do not drive up the road that carries on uphill if the gates are open; these can be locked at any time as it is a private road.

## Approach

From the car park, start walking up the road until you reach where the West Highland Way crosses the road. Follow the WHW left, uphill. Keep following until you reach the forest road at the top. Take a left and walk down to the canyon. When you reach the obvious river, you can either start just by the bridge or if you wish to miss out the

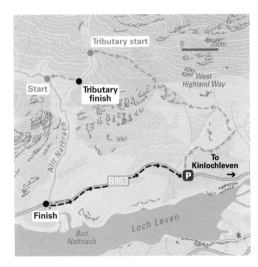

complicated ropework at the start, walk just past the river and take a left following a faint trail down the hillside and enter the canyon just below the last abseil waterfall.

## Descent

Downstream of the bridge is the first abseil, the river splits off to the right, but the best action is on the left flow. The first waterfall has a slippery approach to the second pitch which is a hanging belay around a corner river-left. After this it gets a bit easier with another abseil, then onto some fun jumps. After a little gorge walking it opens out and an obvious exit right can be taken. Hike straight up the riverbank and a rough trail will lead you over the hillside and down to the Nathrach, starting where the river bends right. You can continue down the tributary but there isn't much except one small abseil.

## Water level marker

See details under Nathrach. If the Nathrach is high, the Tributary will be too.

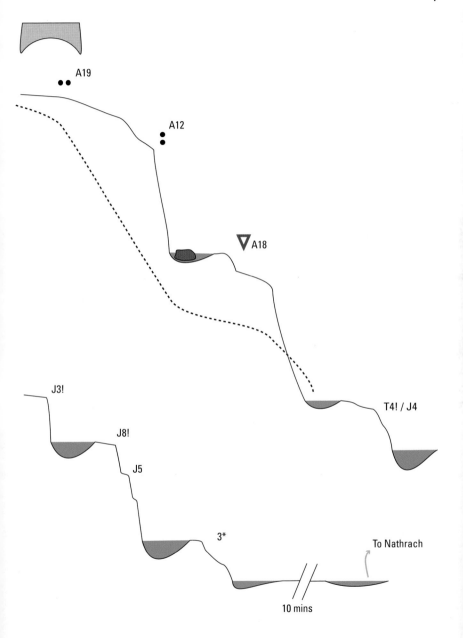

# Nathrach

| Star rating | ★★★ |
|---|---|
| Grade | 3 B/C |
| River | Allt Nathrach |
| Duration | Nathrach Tributary approach – 2 to 3hrs descent – 15mins return |
| Canyon length | 1km |
| Longest abseil | 12m |
| Parking | NN 175 623 (56.7168, -4.9831) |
| In | NN 166 630 (56.7219, -4.9994) |
| Out | NN 166 621 (56.7142, -4.9986) |

## Canyon description

A wonderful and wild Scottish canyon full of excellent slides and plenty of jumps, with a bit or ropework chucked in too. Best to include its tributary. A classic amongst the Scottish canyons.

## Getting there

Please see directions and approach under Nathrach Tributary.

**23**

## Descent

A tricky little downclimb starts this canyon off and some great features follow on from this. A highlight near the start is a toboggan down a smooth slab river-right. The canyon walls steepen up for the start but eventually open out for a lot of beautiful gorge-walking.

You'll eventually reach a brilliant two-tier waterfall, the first tier of which can be jumped from different

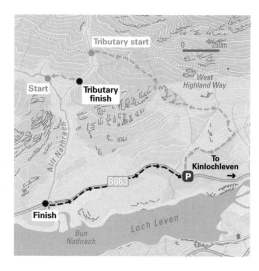

© 'Sending it' big! - The Adventure Photographers

**23**

heights river-right. The next is an awesome aquatic abseil or another daring jump. Take caution jumping into the pool above the abseil in higher flows as you can be washed over the next drop if you're not careful. Downstream of the abseil are some really fun toboggans tucked in a steep-sided gorge.

As you reach the road bridge ahead of you, a small abseil through a hole river-left drops down through a stunning natural archway under the road bridge. Climb out river-right back up to the road and just start walking back towards Kinlochleven.

## Water level marker

You can check the water level quite easily from the road bridge at the end of the canyon. There is a large natural archway where the water passes through which is visible from the road. If it looks as if you could climb through without problems, then it's good to go. If there is quite a bit of flow, then it's maybe too high for beginners. This canyon has a few dangerous hydraulics.

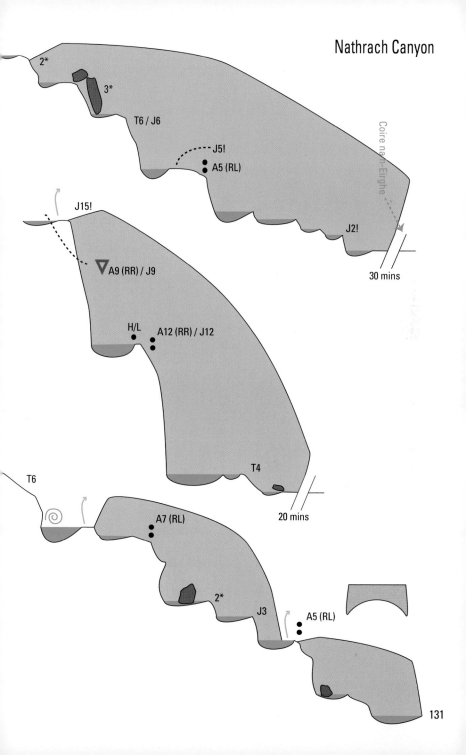

Nathrach Canyon

131

Final pitch - Matt Burden

# Grey Mare's Tail Canyon

| | |
|---|---|
| **Star rating** | ★★★★ |
| **Grade** | 4 B/C |
| **River** | Allt Coire na Ba |
| **Duration** | 35mins approach – 2 to 3hrs descent – 10mins return |
| **Canyon length** | 450m |
| **Longest abseil** | 50m |
| **Parking** | NN 188 623 (56.7167, -4.9627) |
| **In** | NN 189 628 (56.7219, -4.9606) |
| **Out** | NN 188 624 (56.7185, -4.9627) |

## Canyon description

What a canyon! Full of excellent features from top to bottom, gradually getting steeper and deeper as you go along with an epic finish down a huge waterfall. A Scottish classic, often used by a local canyoning company.

## Getting there

Head to Kinlochleven. As you drive into town, head to the north side of the bridge over the River Leven. Now look for a turning which is signposted for Grey Mare's Tail. Turn down this road and drive down to the junction, park in the car park you can see opposite.

## Approach

From the car park, start walking up the footpath following the signs for the waterfall. Pass by a view-point of the fall and down to a wooden bridge. Cross over and turn right, fol-lowing the trail uphill. Keep walking until you reach a split in the path near the top of the treeline. Take the

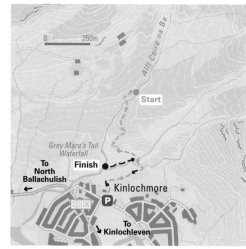

**24**

133

left route alongside the canyon until you reach another footbridge. Either get in by the bridge or walk another 200m upstream and get in by a toboggan feature.

## Descent

If you choose to walk a little further upstream, there are a couple of small fun features before you reach the footbridge. Just below the bridge is a fantastic toboggan (river-left); **watch for an underwater ledge too far left!** Straight after this, a sliding abseil commits you to the canyon. Great features lead you down this brilliant canyon, one slide in this section requires a bit of speed to avoid a small ledge at its base. Eventually you will reach a larger abseil, just after a jump. A guided rappel can be set here to avoid a battering in this aquatic abseil. Before the next smaller abseil, you can use the via feratta here to exit if you require. The 'finale' waterfall goes river-right in two pitches, or three if needed. The ledge for the second pitch is very slippery to access, and the final abseil (50m) has sharp edges!

Once safely in the pool below you can now easily walk downstream to the obvious viewing area and exit the stream. Walk along the path here to the first wooden bridge you crossed on your approach. Cross over and follow the path back to the car park.

## Water level marker

This canyon can rise quite quickly with rain but also drops off quicker than most. A good indicator for the flow is at the small road bridge over the river just a little further along the northern road past the GMT turning. If the rocks in the river are mostly covered the flow is quite high and makes the canyon very difficult and dangerous. You can also gauge the water level by taking a detour on your approach to the exit of the canyon. Here you can easily see the last waterfall and decide if it would be safe to descend.

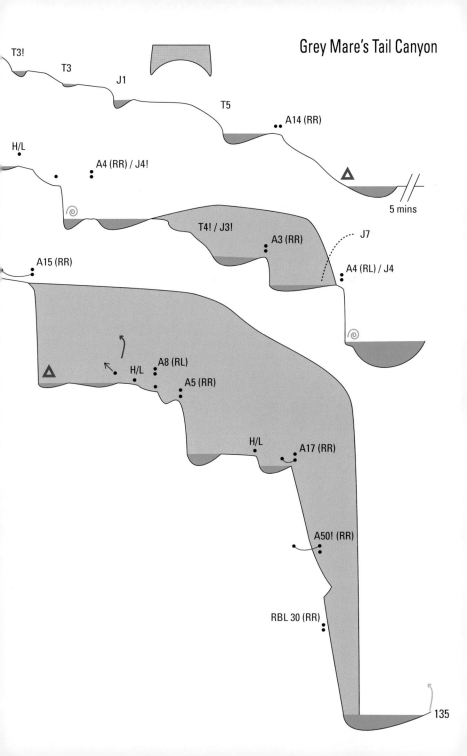

Grey Mare's Tail Canyon

135

📷 Tributary toboggan

# End of the World Gorge

| | |
|---|---|
| **Star rating** | ★★ |
| **Grade** | 2 B/C |
| **River** | River Leven |
| **Duration** | 30mins approach – 1hr descent |
| **Canyon length** | 1km |
| **Longest abseil** | 10m (optional) |
| **Parking** | NN 189 619 (56.7140, -4.9612) |
| **In** | NN 202 613 (56.7087, -4.9391) |
| **Out** | NN 194 618 (56.7127, -4.9524) |

## Canyon description

A superb gorge-walk. The series of waterfalls make a great journey for those wanting to forgo the complications of ropework and enjoy being in a river. Should you want to practise however, there are plenty of options to build an abseil. There is a bonus to this route on a tributary river - Scotland's longest toboggan, at just under 20m!

## Getting there

Drive to Kinlochleven, and head to Ice Factor in the middle of town. Park in the car park here.

## Approach

From Ice Factor, begin walking along the road towards the Blackwater Hostel where there are camping pods. Walk past these and follow the road to a blue bridge over the river. Take a right after the bridge and past a hydro building, following the gravel track uphill. Not far up this track you need to take a right, marked the

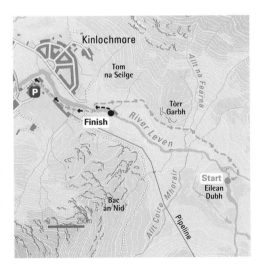

© Nice jumps

Ciaran path. Follow this track upstream for about 15–20mins. When you cross over a stream on a footbridge, begin to veer right off the path towards the river. Get in here. Alternatively, if you wish to enjoy an awesome toboggan first, as you cross this last footbridge, begin to walk upstream of the river you crossed. Stay on the river-right side, climbing up higher past the first feature until you can see the toboggan.

## Descent

If you start at the amazing toboggan, you can enjoy a few goes here before making your way back to the main gorge. Now in the River Leven, you can play in a few small rapids before the waterfalls begin to drop you into the gorge. If you brought a rope, you can set-up a few abseils down these waterfalls. Otherwise, start to downclimb and scramble along the rocks. There are some good jumps dotted around, but do check first, some pools are deceptively shallow. After this series of waterfalls, the river flows gently through a beautiful steep-sided gorge before another large waterfall. Climb down the centre; a jump is possible but there are some boulders underwater. After this, small rapids and more swimming eventually bring you back to the blue bridge. Exit here and walk back to the car.

## Water level marker

You can check the flow of this gorge by the camping pods. As you look at the river here, there should be a lot of rocks visible in the riverbed. If the majority of them are covered or the river is flowing quite rapidly, the gorge will be too dangerous to descend. Time to grab your kayak and the *Scottish White Water* guidebook instead.

25

Short abseils – The Adventure Photographers

Slip 'n' Slide

# Van Halen Gorge

| Star rating | ★★ |
| --- | --- |
| Grade | 2/3 B/C |
| River | Allt Gleann a'Chaolais |
| Duration | 20mins approach – 1hr to 1hr 30mins descent |
| Canyon length | 450m |
| Longest abseil | 12m |
| Parking | NN 142 608 (56.7014, -5.0357) |
| In | NN 145 605 (56.6991, -5.0309) |
| Out | NN 143 607 (56.7013, -5.0353) |

## Canyon description

A fun wee gorge full of spectacular toboggans. This is a short trip but a great addition to the other canyons in the Loch Leven area. A perfect gorge for beginners and fun for the experienced too.

## Getting there

Three miles from Kinlochleven on the southern road, just before you reach Caolasnacon campsite, you will cross a small road bridge over the gorge. Park in the left or right layby just next to the bridge.

## Approach

Cross the bridge to walk uphill on the river-right side. Follow a boggy trail all the way up until the river starts to flatten out. You should see a deer fence end on the opposite side of the river, enter the river just upstream of this where the river is flat.

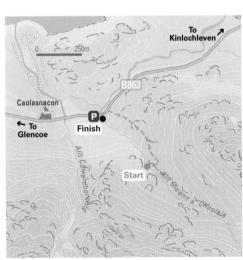

📷 Great toboggan

**26**

## Descent

The features in this canyon are fairly obvious and you will find the majority of them are toboggans, but always take care and check. Not too far from the start is a steeper drop that requires an abseil but can be avoided by climbing down river-left. More fun features follow this until another abseil feature which can be carefully downclimbed or walked around. Some more gorge-walking leads you down to the most impressive toboggan, then on to a slot for some bridging action, but this can be avoided by climbing around the river-left side.

Just a couple of features more and then the very last waterfall finishes with a toboggan before the bridge. Clamber out river-left to your vehicle.

## Water level marker

Walk up to the top of the last set of waterfalls seen from the road bridge. A man-made concrete platform with water running over it should be visible. In this concrete are several re-bar ends protruding up. If these ends are creating rooster tails then the level is roughly medium flow, a great level for the slides. If these re-bar ends are completely covered then the level is potentially too high but the gorge can be descended by experienced white-water canyoneers.

# Van Halen Gorge

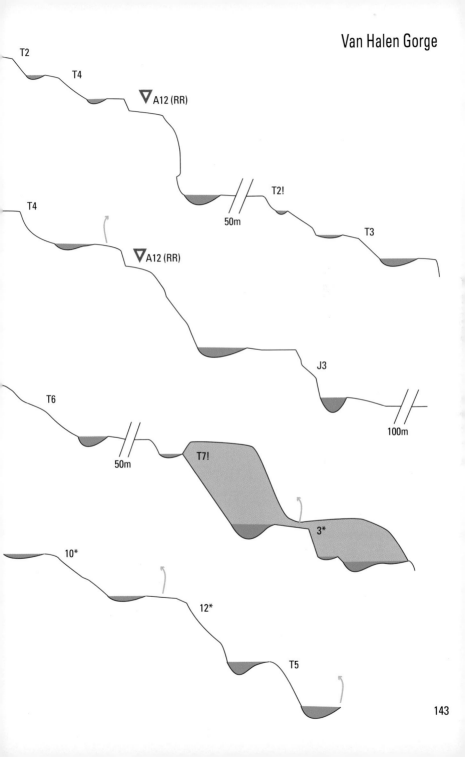

# Duror Canyon

| Star rating | ★ |
| --- | --- |
| Grade | 4 A |
| River | Eas a' Choin |
| Duration | 30min / 50mins approach – 1hr descent |
| Canyon length | 250m |
| Longest abseil | 38m |
| Parking | NN 002 563 (56.6556, -5.2610) |
| In | NN 009 563 (56.6558, -5.2490) |
| Out | NN 007 563 (56.6562, -5.2519) |

## Canyon description

A short adventurous canyon with sculpted waterfalls and the daring cairn anchor requirement for the main waterfall. This is a great canyon for those wanting to practise more advanced canyon techniques.

## Getting there

Driving south from Ballachulish on the A828 towards Oban you will pass through a small village called Kentallen. Less than a mile past the village is the Kentallen and Duror Community Centre on the right-hand side. Park in the car park here. Please be considerate when changing.

## Approach

Cross over the road and follow the path through some blue posts. Turn left at the bottom and follow the bike path along until you reach a farm gate on your right, beside a cottage. Cross over this gate and head uphill towards the canyon. Now either follow faint trails up to the quarry for the faster

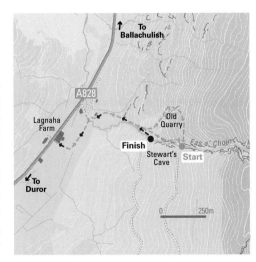

approach or start traversing around the hillside, which takes longer. If you choose the quarry route then you will need good climbing ability as it gets steep, scrambling up the right side corner closest to the river. Near the top it will become obvious where you can easily access the canyon. You know you're in the right spot if you see some metal girders in the river from an old dam.

If you have traversed left, under the quarry and walked up the hillside then you may access the canyon further uphill and you'll find a few more small abseils to contend with.

## Descent

Unless you hiked further uphill, the first abseil has bolts on the right but beware of a sharp edge over the waterfall lip. At the base of this waterfall is a small dry cave you can walk into. The next waterfall abseil drops you down to the main event. This large waterfall requires a cairn anchor to be built in order to abseil down; take great care. A difficult escape out river-right may be possible if needed. Successfully navigating this waterfall, you can now scramble your way down and out of the canyon, following your approach route back to the car.

## Water level marker

**27**

This canyon usually has low flow but could go in higher flows. However, the cairn anchor pitch would be dangerously difficult. You can get a glimpse of the waterfalls through the trees; if they look full and white then it is too high. The stream below should not be very full at all.

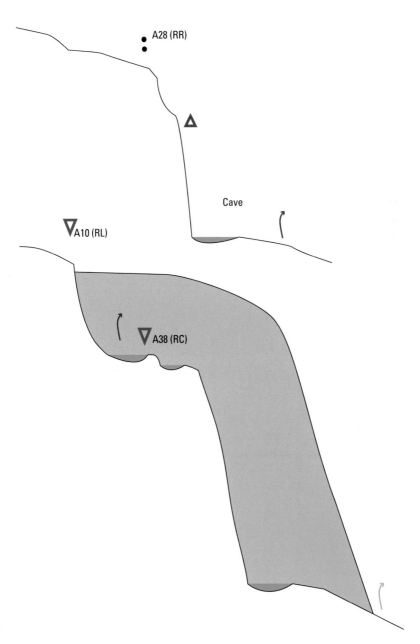

A28 (RR)

Cave

A10 (RL)

A38 (RC)

Bidean Falls

# Bidean Falls

| Star rating | ★★ |
|---|---|
| Grade | 4 A/B |
| River | Allt Coire nam Beithach |
| Duration | 1hr approach – 2hrs descent – 20mins return |
| Canyon length | 300m |
| Longest abseil | 38m |
| Parking | NN 139 567 (56.6646, -5.0388) |
| In | NN 141 557 (56.6560, -5.0344) |
| Out | NN 140 560 (56.6585, -5.0363) |

## Canyon description

A stunning canyon location over-looking the magnificent Glen Coe. It starts high up in open waterfalls and then descends into a more enclosed finish. There are natural anchors all the way down.

## Getting there

**28**

This one is rather easy to spot as you drive down the road into Glen Coe. Heading south on the A82 from Glen Coe village you will soon spot a series of waterfalls on the mountainside ahead. There is a large layby just off the road by a bridge, situated next to Loch Achtriochtan.
Park here.

## Approach

Walk out of the layby and cross over the road bridge to the river-left side. Do not walk over the wooden bridge towards the house. Just on the other side of the road bridge is a path to your left. Start following this path towards the canyon. Follow the trail as it zigzags its way up the hill

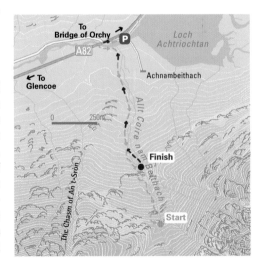

📷 Lower gorge

past all the waterfalls. As the path starts to turn into the coire, make your way down to the river above all the action.

## Descent

Starting in an open riverbed, make your way towards the first few abseils. There are plenty of boulders to anchor off. The abseils gradually get bigger until the largest waterfall, which you may have seen from the road. A huge rock spike gives a good anchor for this one, but it can be hard to retrieve your rope. After this it's just an open stream, best to walk alongside this until you reach the next set of abseils that descend into the trees. There is nothing too complicated ahead, with lots of natural anchors. When you finally make it out of the trees at the end just follow the trail back down to the car park below.

## Water level marker

You can gauge the flow from the very bottom by just looking up towards the gorge. Looking at the largest fall on the hillside, if this looks like a broken spray of water it's low whereas if there's a lot of white water it may be too high.

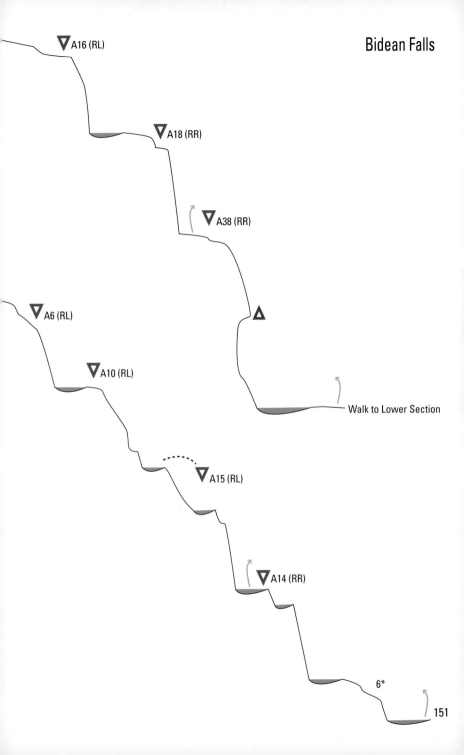

A16 (RL)

A18 (RR)

A38 (RR)

A6 (RL)

A10 (RL)

Walk to Lower Section

A15 (RL)

A14 (RR)

6*

Rhian dropping in.

# Upper Coe Gorge

| | |
|---|---|
| **Star rating** | ★★ |
| **Grade** | 3 B/C |
| **River** | Allt Lairig Eilde into River Coe |
| **Duration** | 30mins approach – 2hrs descent - 15mins return |
| **Canyon length** | 1.3km |
| **Longest abseil** | 15m |
| **Parking** | NN 184 563 (56.6628, -4.9651) |
| **In** | NN 182 557 (56.6580, -4.9670) |
| **Out** | NN 176 565 (56.6643, -4.9776) |

## Canyon description

An awesome stream to play around in if you're in the Glen Coe area. A special hanging-drop feature makes the journey worthwhile. This upper section of gorge is not to be confused with the kayaking section also called Coe Gorge, downstream of Loch Achtriochtan.

## Getting there

Drive out of Glen Coe village into Glen Coe heading towards the ski resort. Once you go past the Three Sisters mountains, you will reach a waterfall viewpoint directly beside the road on a left bend. This is it. Park in a layby just next to the viewing area.

## Approach

Start to walk up over the verge by the road and follow a trail that leads to the top of the roadside waterfall. You can cut your journey short and start climbing down the water-fall here or keep walking upstream on river-right until the river starts to flatten out. You will see a lot of the features along the way.

📷 Glen Coe

### Descent

You can begin your descent anywhere upstream of the main falls. Upstream of the roadside waterfall you will find some small fun slides and jumps to play around in as you descend. The one larger waterfall in the upper section has very few anchors for an abseil but can be avoided by climbing around it. The main waterfall by the road also has no anchors for an abseil so you will need to climb down this one.

After this the river flows into the gorge that drops below the road and this is where you'll find some interesting features. One of these is a drop / jump into a slot on river-left which is pretty tight. Following the crystal green water down, you will find one abseil from natural anchors in this gorge. The remaining canyon flows through small steep-sided slots with little jumps dotted around.

Eventually the river opens out and finishes with a large deep pool where there are a variety of jump heights to choose from. After you've had your fill of jumps just walk up towards the road and back along to your vehicle.

### Water level marker

You can easily gauge the flow from the road by checking the waterfall right there. This canyon will go in most flows but in higher flows the gorge below will be very pushy and dangerous. The waterfall should not be flowing over the slab at the top; for a good level the flow should be dropping into the slot.

Log jam in the lower gorge

Aquatic abseil

# Sutherland's Grove Gorge

| | |
|---|---|
| **Star rating** | ★★ |
| **Grade** | 3 B |
| **River** | Abhainn Teithil |
| **Duration** | 30mins approach – 2hrs descent – 10mins return |
| **Canyon length** | 1.1km (including lower gorge) |
| **Longest abseil** | 12m |
| **Parking** | NM 966 422 (56.5276, -5.3089) |
| **In** | NM 976 423 (56.5289, -5.2930) |
| **Finish** | NM 972 421 (56.5273, -5.2997) |
| **Lower finish** | NM 967 420 (56.5264, -5.3076) |

### Canyon description

Magnificently carved rock walls covered in moss and ferns make this an exceptionally beautiful gorge to descend. Not overly challenging but definitely the most slippery gorge in Scotland.

### Getting there

Driving north from Oban on the A82 towards Fort William, cross over the Connel Bridge and continue along the A82 for just under 8 miles. As you pass through the small village of Barcaldine and drive out the other side, look for the forestry sign on your right with Sutherland's Grove marked on it. Pull in here and park in the car park near the stone bridge over the river.

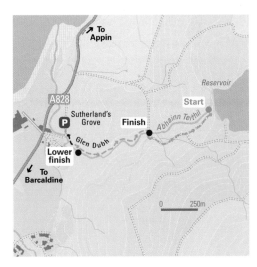

### Approach

Head up the trail beside the river on river-right and continue walking until you reach a footbridge. You do not want to cross this bridge, but you can walk onto it to get a view of the lower gorge section. Instead, at the stairs down to the footbridge, climb up left and continue on the trail upstream river-right. When you reach the forest road bridge cross over and turn left and continue to walk up the forest road on river-left. At a split, take a left and eventually you will reach the dam. Get in just below the dam.

## Descent

Starting your descent from the outflow of the reservoir, you will begin to gorge-walk down a gentle river and soon realise why Sutherland's is known for being the most slippery. A couple of jumps near the start then gorge-walking and downclimbing until you reach the first abseil. The bolts are high up on the right above a natural rock arch. There is the option to drop into the pool just below the bolts, but it can be tricky to climb up to them for the next abseil. This abseil brings you down onto natural debris suspended above the water, with the option to jump off this debris or abseil all the way down. Now surrounded by carved walls, some more gorge-walking leads you out and down to the next abseil. Here you will find two anchor stations, the left is aquatic, and the right is drier. Once you can see the forest road bridge you can make an exit here and walk back down.

If you choose to continue on past this bridge you will reach the lower gorge section. Here you will find small drops and downclimbing through more beautifully carved walls, maybe with a few tourists watching from above. Exit out right when the river flattens out.

## Water level marker

This gorge has a reservoir above it that has a bell-mouth overflow. It is a good idea to check the level of the loch when you reach the top to give you an indication of how likely it is that water will flow over and into the canyon. However, be aware that there are also maintenance pipes below that can release water without warning.

To check the levels of the river at the car park, look into the stream at the bridge. If the rocks in the river are mostly covered then it's high. Ideally you want a gentle stream flowing under the bridge.

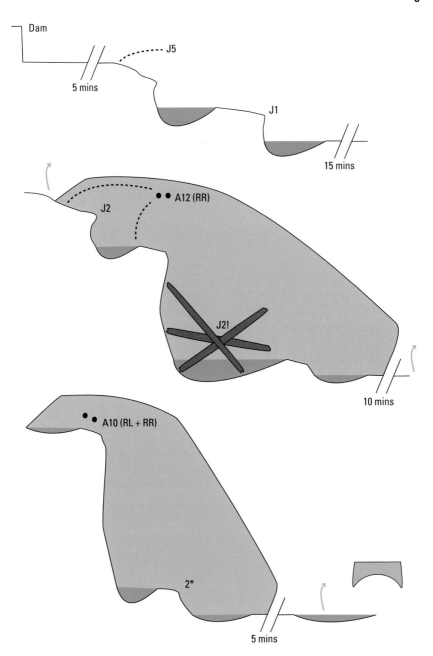

The Falls of Bruar (Route 31) - The Adventure Photograp

# Central

Probably the most popular destination for canyoning because of the brilliant classics it has to offer. Bruar Falls is the most descended canyon in Scotland, and rightly so as you'll find out. But that's not the only classic here. In this central area of Scotland, the canyons are a bit more forgiving than some of those in the North or West, making this a great place to start if you are new to the sport.

# Bruar Falls – Upper

| Star rating | ★★ |
| --- | --- |
| Grade | 3 B |
| River | Bruar Water |
| Duration | 40mins approach – 40mins descent |
| Canyon length | 450m |
| Longest abseil | 25m |
| Parking | NN 820 659 (56.7698, -3.9323) |
| In | NN 820 669 (56.7787, -3.9327) |
| Out | NN 819 665 (56.7754, -3.9340) |

## Canyon description

Probably the most popular canyon in Scotland. This upper section contains a spectacular waterfall that plunges into a deep pool below. A superb day of canyoning when combined with the lower section.

## Getting there

See Bruar Falls – Lower for details.

**31**

## Approach

Keep heading up the trail from the first stone bridge for another 15-20mins to the upper Bruar waterfall. You will have a good view of the fall on your way up. When you reach another stone footbridge, cross over and get in on the upstream side.

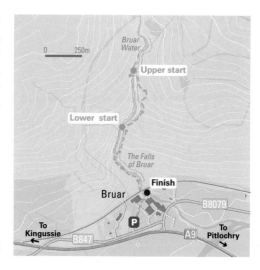

## Descent

You can start off a few different ways at the first

© Down the big one – The Adventure Photographers

**31** feature of the canyon – there's a variety of jumps or slides. A few smaller drops lead you down to the main waterfall. A handline traverse around to a bolt station lines up the abseil straight down into the pool below. In higher flows, being behind this fall can be troublesome and requires strong swimming to exit. There are guided rappel bolts on the opposite wall if required. There is a hidden ledge a few metres down the abseil that offers a bold jump, but inspection is required as there is a large rock shelf under the water! After all this it is just simple gorge-walking until you finally reach the lower section of the canyon.

### Water level marker

See Bruar Falls – Lower for details.

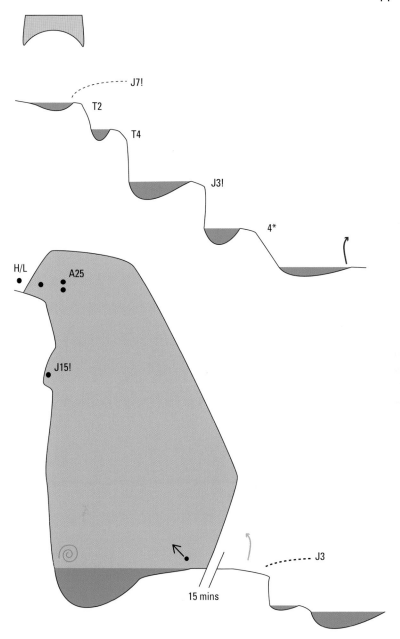

J7!

T2

T4

J3!

4*

H/L

A25

J15!

J3

15 mins

# Bruar Falls – Lower

| | |
|---|---|
| **Star rating** | ★★★ |
| **Grade** | 2 B |
| **River** | Bruar Water |
| **Duration** | 25mins approach – 1hr 30mins descent – 5mins return |
| **Canyon length** | 550m |
| **Longest abseil** | 7m |
| **Parking** | NN 820 659 (56.7698, -3.9323) |
| **In** | NN 819 665 (56.7754, -3.9340) |
| **Out** | NN 821 661 (56.7717, -3.9310) |

## Canyon description

A brilliant section of canyon all on its own but even better when combined with the upper section. Smooth water-carved rock and crystal waters make this a beautiful canyoning playground. Popular with canyoning companies.

## Getting there

Driving north on the A9 out of Pitlochry for just over 10 miles, you will reach the House of Bruar, a shopping centre. You can park in the left car park here but please park on the far side away from the mall and be considerate when changing. There have been problems before, and we do not want to ruin the canyoning relationship with them.

## Approach

Walk towards the House of Bruar shopping mall and take the path up left that goes behind and starts following the river upstream. You will reach a stone bridge, crossing the canyon, and from here you can see some of the canyon features you'll explore. Head uphill for about 200m

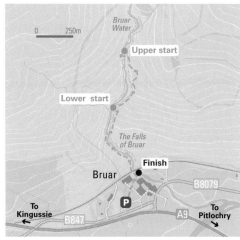

Jumping in – The Adventure Photographers

more then turn towards the canyon through some spaced-out trees. An obvious steep track leads you down to the canyon.

## Descent

**32**

You can either start your descent with a small jump-in here or a larger jump can be made from the top, before you climb down to the canyon. Check the depth first. The following features are usually descended on river-right until you reach the bridge again but there are options river-left. A great 'slide to drop' feature can be found just before the bridge. Under the bridge, there are handline bolts to protect against getting washed over as you approach a short abseil. If you'd like to skip the abseil, exit left and cross the bridge to river-right then climb back down to the rock arch.

In the remainder of the canyon you will find some small slides, jumps and plenty of interesting gorge-walking. The gorge walls are steep but, in an emergency, exit is possible either river-right or left in places. As you walk under the railway bridge, climb out right to gain access to the car park.

## Water level marker

A hydro scheme controls the flow in this river. There are two dams, miles upstream of this river and they can release automatically without warning! You can check the flow of the river just before the first footbridge you cross. The waterfall that flows before the rock arch should look like a spray of water; if this is a thick brown flow then the canyon is too high. For more information on the current dam conditions contact a local canyoning company.

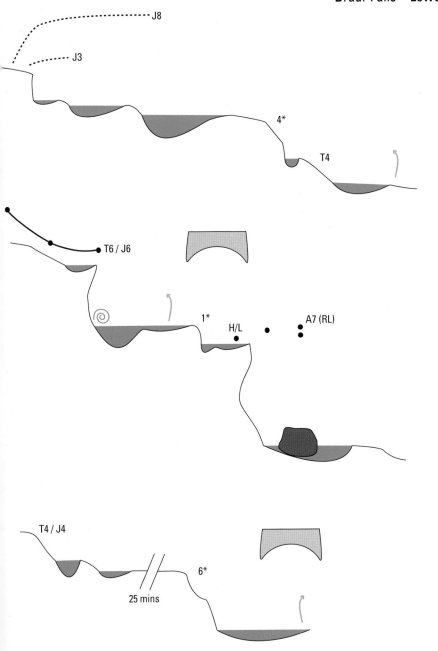

Sliding into action - The Adventure Photograp

# Tummel Canyon

| | |
|---|---|
| **Star rating** | ★★ |
| **Grade** | 4 A/B |
| **River** | Allt Aird Raineach |
| **Duration** | 30mins approach – 1.5 to 2hrs descent |
| **Canyon length** | 450m |
| **Longest abseil** | 22m |
| **Parking** | NN 843 592 (56.7104, -3.8908) |
| **In** | NN 845 588 (56.7066, -3.8882) |
| **Out** | NN 843 592 (56.7102, -3.8911) |

## Canyon description

Tucked away along the side of Loch Tummel is this steep little canyon with some excellent abseiling. The canyon itself is well equipped with most pitches having anchors on both sides; this is because it is used as a training venue by a local canyoning company. The canyon is not too committing, which makes this a great place to practise your own skills.

## Getting there

Head north from Dunkeld on the A9, driving towards Pitlochry. Continue on the A9 past the turning for Pitlochry. After a few miles, look for a turning right, signposted for Clunie. Turn down here and follow the road around and under the A9. Follow this single-track road for roughly 7 miles. Driving alongside Loch Tummel, you will reach a layby on the left, next to a small stone bridge and a wild camping area to the right. Park here.

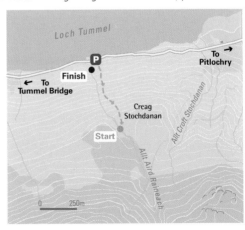

## Approach

Start hiking uphill on the river-right side. Follow a faint trail up through the trees until the river starts to level out. Get in above the waterfalls you can clearly see.

Managing the flow – The Adventure Photographers

### Descent

The canyon starts off as it means to go on, with abseiling. There are handline bolts available if you require them. Once in, the fun begins. Navigate your way down some fun and often aquatic waterfalls and before long you will have descended quickly to one of the larger pitches with gorgeous views out to Loch Tummel. A beautiful two-tiered waterfall drops you down into a small, hard to escape, pool above an impressive and aquatic 22m pitch. After this abseil the canyon leads down into more short abseils before descending into an awesome steep-sided gorge. Take care in higher flows as this pitch can be quite pushy. Just a few more abseil pitches bring you down near the road where you can easily exit the river and head back to your vehicle.

### Water level marker

The water level can be easily gauged from the road at the bottom. Looking into the stream you ideally want a calm stream flowing among the rocks. If the riverbed looks quite full some of the pitches become full-on, but can be still be descended with caution by an experienced canyoneer. If the stream is fast flowing and turning brown then it is too high.

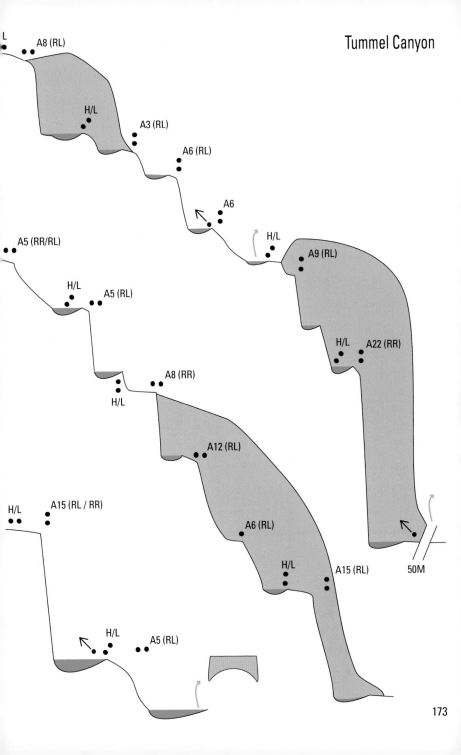

Tummel Canyon

173

# Falls of Acharn

| | |
|---|---|
| **Star rating** | ★★ |
| **Grade** | 3 A – C |
| **River** | Acharn Burn |
| **Duration** | 20mins approach – 1hr 30min descent |
| **Canyon length** | 750m |
| **Longest abseil** | 25m |
| **Parking** | NN 757 437 (56.5690, -4.0254) |
| **In** | NN 758 430 (56.5625, -4.0226) |
| **Out** | NN 756 437 (56.5685, -4.0253) |

## Canyon description

Short and sweet! A canyon with some great features. The smooth 6m toboggan that narrows at the end is quite the thrill. With easy access and escape possible throughout, this is a great canyon to start out on. However, when in full flow this becomes a daring canyon for the experienced canyoneer.

## Getting there

**34**

Head to the small town of Kenmore on the shores of Loch Tay. As you reach Kenmore coming from Aberfeldy on the A827 there is a steep right-hand turn towards the town; here you need to turn left to take a road on the south side of Loch Tay. Follow this for 1.5 miles and you'll reach the small village of Acharn. Turn left into the village, passing an old red phonebooth. Park off the road, by the playground. Do not block the farm gate.

## Approach

Walk straight up the path ahead of you that follows

alongside the river. Near the top is a wooden bridge crossing the canyon that gives you a good vantage point for the amazing slide. Walk further uphill and you'll meet a track that goes over an old stone bridge, get in above this bridge.

## Descent

The first feature, downstream of the stone bridge, can be jumped but be careful not to land too close to the wall. Some slippery downclimbing (easiest river-left) leads you to the top of the toboggan. Keep your elbows in as it narrows at the end. The pool here is quite deep and if you fancy a thrill, it has been jumped into from a variety of spots.

After this, some gorge-walking and a short abseil brings you to the top of the main event. Be careful approaching the pitch head in high flows as it is easy to get washed over. There are now two options. Either abseil down this amazing sliding abseil, river-right down the smooth slab or river-left down an awesome slide to a slot lower down. At this point, you can either make a steep escape up the bank river-right or choose to carry on downstream.

From here, there is a short abseil before downclimbing and easy gorge-walking with another small abseil towards the end. Exit river-right at the pump house.

## 34 Water level marker

This river has a hydro scheme on it. Water is taken out further uphill of the canyon which means it is typically low and a good option when most other canyons are too high. A good place to check the water level is at the wooden bridge. If the slide has a trickle of water, then it's low. If it has good amount of water, then it's high and certain parts of the canyon can be very hydraulic, only the more experienced canyoneer may want to tackle it in these conditions. If the slide is white water and the pool below is turbulent do not descend.

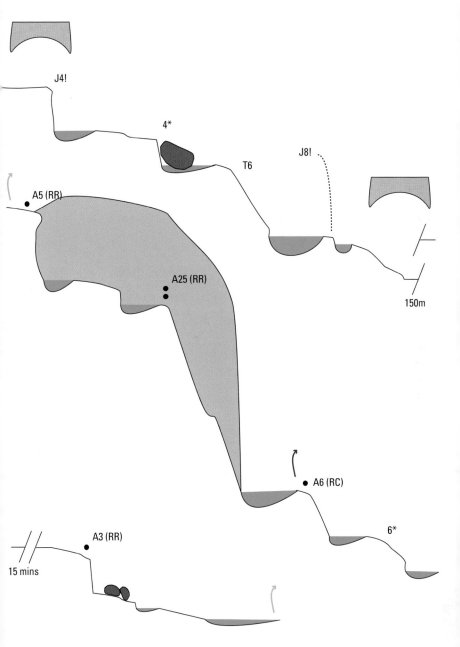

J4!

4*

J8!

T6

A5 (RR)

A25 (RR)

150m

A6 (RC)

6*

A3 (RR)

15 mins

# The Birks

| Star rating | ★★ |
|---|---|
| Grade | 4 B |
| River | Moness Burn |
| Duration | 45mins approach – 2hrs descent – 15mins return |
| Canyon length | 700m (excluding the Lower Birks) |
| Longest abseil | 20m |
| Parking | NN 855 486 (56.6156, -3.8665) |
| In | NN 852 472 (56.6029, -3.8720) |
| Out | NN 853 477 (56.6071, -3.8707) |

## Canyon description

This green canyon runs straight down to the town of Aberfeldy. A cool place to be and possibly the quickest return to a pub afterwards. The canyon is currently fine to explore but it is protected as part of the SSSI.

## Getting there

**35**

Drive to the town of Aberfeldy on the A827 off the A9. As you drive into town, keep going along the road towards Kenmore. At the traffic lights on the west side of town, take a left turn up towards the Birks. Park in the car park at the bottom marked the Birks o' Aberfeldy. It's possible to do a shuttle up to the top via the Urlar road, taking the left turn at the split. Not far past this turning you will need to park a car in a grass layby next to a field.

## Approach

From the bottom car park, follow the well-marked trail up either side of the river to the footbridge at the top, which runs over the first waterfall.

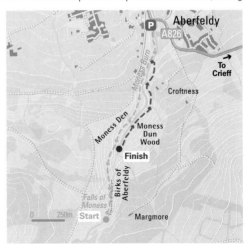

© Handlining – The Adventure Photographers

If you did a shuttle, a pathway opposite the layby in the woods will lead you down to the footbridge.

## Descent

**35**

To start your descent of this canyon, set-up an abseil either side the bridge. Please try to leave no trace! Now committing to the descent, some tricky downclimbing and gorge-walking lead you into the gorge to the next abseil. The waterfall after this requires you to climb down the left to handline bolts. Make your way along river-left to reach the anchors for a sweet abseil down. A couple more features bring you down to an old disused walkway. Here a waterfall drops away to the left and this drop has been jumped, inspection required.

The old walkway can be used to exit if you do not want to commit for the next few hundred metres. After a short tight section, the river opens out and an easy exit river-right can be taken up to the path. Follow this path back down the river to the car park.

The Lower Birks contain only low-angle waterfalls and good, more simple gorge-walking, but a few fun slides can be found if you care to explore.

## Water level marker

You can check out the flows for this canyon at the Lower Birks which run through the village. If most of the rocks are covered in the stream, the canyon is very high and only experienced canyoneers should attempt descent. If the stream is full it is too high!

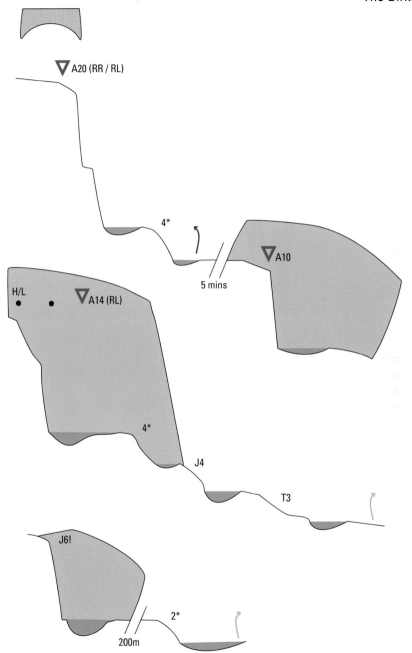

# Dalguise Gorge

| | |
|---|---|
| **Star rating** | ★ |
| **Grade** | 2/3 A |
| **River** | Milton Burn |
| **Duration** | 10mins approach / return – 1hr 30mins ascent – 1hr descent |
| **Canyon length** | 600m |
| **Longest abseil** | 20m |
| **Parking** | NN 991 486 (56.6188, -3.6457) |
| **In / out (bottom)** | NN 988 486 (56.6187, -3.6514) |
| **In / out (top)** | NN 982 486 (56.6179, -3.6602) |

## Canyon description

A hidden little gem in the heart of Scotland. This route is described for both ascent and descent. The gorge is packed full of low-angled waterfalls and a small steep-sided gorge in a short distance of river.

## Getting there

Heading north from Dunkeld on the A9, take a left turn just before the road crosses over the River Tay. It will be signposted for Dalguise. Drive down this road until you pass the signs for PGL Dalguise. Continue along for a few hundred metres more, passing a farmhouse on your left, until you see a cottage beside a small road bridge. There is a small spot on the right, directly opposite the cottage, to park one vehicle. Make sure not to obstruct the farm access and leave room for a passing place.

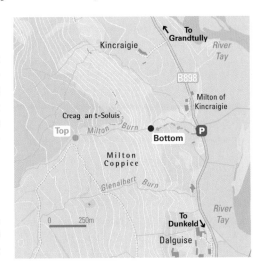

## Approach

From the parking spot, cross over a fence into the field to the left of the

Hidden little falls

cottage. Walk up the field until you reach the tree line at the back and cross a gate to the right. Make your way towards the river on your right and access the gorge here.

## Ascent / descent

Starting at the first waterfall you can begin carefully climbing your way up these waterfalls. For the less experienced climber, it would be smart to treat these like lead climbing by placing protection and using belays. There is a small section of gorge halfway up that may be full of debris and can be easily avoided by walking around river-left beside a stone wall. As the waterfalls get smaller you will eventually reach the top. Turn around and descend the route back down to the car. There are plenty of natural anchors in place to set-up abseils to make a safer journey down.

There is a forest road at the top of the canyon that can be used to access/exit the canyon. Using a map, you will see it leads back down to Dalmarnock forestry car park.

## Water level marker

From the parking spot you can get a rough gauge of the river levels by looking into the river but it is best to gauge at the bottom waterfall. It is good to go in most flows as long as it is not a brown mess of water rushing down. In higher flows it may be dangerous to ascend and should only be descended instead.

Drover's Falls (Route 41)

# Southern

Let's head south a bit, but not too south. This area of Scotland has two main areas for canyoning, Loch Lomond and the Trossachs national park and the Ochill Hills. At the base of the Ochill Hills you'll find two great classic – Alva and Dollar, very different but brilliant trips. Around the Trossachs you'll find a great variety of canyons from steep big waterfalls to small deep slots and more.

# Cruachan Canyon

| Star rating | ★★★ |
|---|---|
| Grade | 4+ A |
| River | Allt Cruachan |
| Duration | 30mins approach – 2 to 3hrs descent – 5mins return |
| Canyon length | 600m |
| Longest abseil | 23m |
| Parking | NN 081 267 (56.3935, -5.1114) |
| In | NN 081 274 (56.3992, -5.1109) |
| Out | NN 078 268 (56.3945, -5.1142) |

## Canyon description

This vegetated, boulder-strewn canyon has some intriguing features to abseil and a spectacularly deep gorge section. It's generally low in water as the dam above takes out most of the flow.

## Getting there

From Tyndrum, follow the A85 for about 18 miles until you reach the Falls of Cruachan train station beside the Cruachan Hollow Mountain experience. Park in the dirt layby beside the train station.

From Oban, head north to Connel Bridge on the A82 but do not go over the bridge. Instead go under it by continuing along the A85 to the Cruachan car park described above.

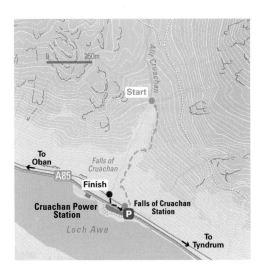

## Approach

Start by walking under the railway through a small footpath tunnel. Follow the footpath that leads off up the hillside, following the canyon's side. After a steep

📷 Matt free-hanging

hike, you will eventually reach a deer fence. Once you pass through this, hike just a little further before walking down to the river where it is easy to access.

### Descent

**37**

The majority of this canyon involves abseiling and the starting abseil anchor can be found up on the right. Uncomplicated but enjoyable, sometimes aquatic, abseils descend steeply down off Ben Cruachan. There are a few downclimbs but they could be rigged for abseils instead. As you approach the steep gorge you will find escape is possible beforehand.

In the gorge you will find anchor rigging becomes a little trickier. A small abseil, river-left, drops you onto a giant boulder platform with a superb overhanging abseil for the next pitch. Be careful with your rope as there is a sharp edge and a choke can make rope-retrieval problematic. Another beautiful pitch finishes the gorge section then a short gorge walk brings you around to the last abseil.

As you approach the end you will see the road in front and the train bridge above. The tunnel you see leads to Loch Awe but there is no path at the end of the tunnel. Climb out river-right under the bridge and walk back along the road to your vehicle.

### Water level marker

The Cruachan hydro scheme above this burn takes out most of the flow from the canyon. However, there is clear evidence of high water passing through the canyon so be aware. You can easily check the flow from looking into the canyon from the road where you would exit. There should be a gentle stream. If it is white water then do not descend.

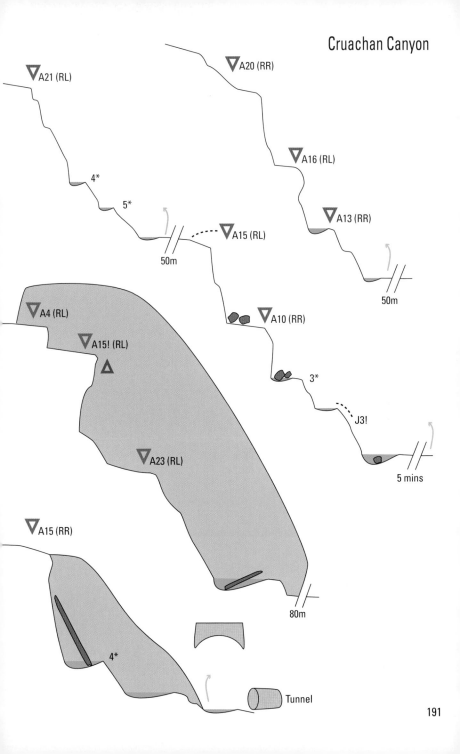

Cruachan Canyon

A21 (RL)

A20 (RR)

A16 (RL)

4*

5*

A15 (RL)

A13 (RR)

50m

50m

A4 (RL)

A10 (RR)

A15! (RL)

3*

J3!

A23 (RL)

5 mins

A15 (RR)

80m

4*

Tunnel

Andy in the shower

# Eagle's Canyon – Upper

| | |
|---|---|
| **Star rating** | ★★★ |
| **Grade** | 4+ A/B |
| **River** | Eas an Tuirc |
| **Duration** | 1hr 30mins approach – 1hr 30mins descent |
| **Canyon length** | 750m (including gorge walk to lower) |
| **Longest abseil** | 34m |
| **Parking** | NN 193 128 (56.2729, -4.9192) |
| **In** | NN 227 142 (56.2875, -4.8657) |
| **Out** | NN 221 145 (56.2895, -4.8759) |

## Canyon description

This section of canyon sits high up in the hills of Glen Fyne. Although short, this is a committing and remote descent into a steep slot canyon which will reward you with brilliant abseils. Combined with the lower canyon this is a very big day of canyoning.

## Getting there

Drive along the A82 beside Loch Lomond and take the turning at Tarbet to head towards Arrochar on the A83. Passing through Arrochar, continue along this road to reach Cairndow. Just along the A83 past Cairndow, take a turning right shortly before

**38**

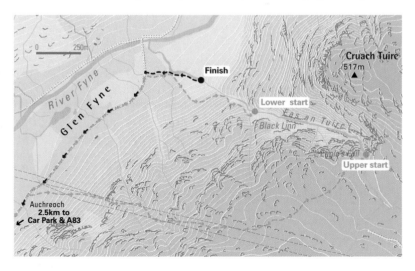

the road bridge – signposted for the Fyne Ales Brewery. On this road, take the first left over a smaller road bridge then left again into a car park. Park here.

## Approach

Walk back over the small bridge spanning the River Fyne. Take a left, walking towards the brewery. Keep walking along this road for about 30mins. Eventually you will reach a line of pylons that climb up the hillside to your right. Follow these pylons up the steep hillside, you may find faint trails to use. As you near the top the two lines of pylons split into three, at this point, start to veer left towards the river. The top of the slot canyon will become obvious as you approach it. Enter the river by climbing down river-left.

## Descent

The starting abseil drops you into the steep-sided slot straight away but be careful here as the rope can prove difficult to retrieve due to a few tight grooves on the lip. The next abseil anchors can be found on top of the large boulder choke and this is the most impressive waterfall. Watch where you come off at the end of the rope as there is a sump to pass at the base of the fall. It is better to try and land on top of the chockstone creating the sump, or abseil past it on the downstream side to avoid the hazard. Following this are a few more abseils until you reach the bottom and begin the long gorge-walk to the lower canyon section.

## Water level marker

Unfortunately there are no places from which to view this river unless you walk another 15mins along the road to check the river at the base. However, along the walk-in, on the road, you are able to view all the other tributary rivers to the River Fyne that pour down the sides of the glen. If these small rivers are running rather white then the canyon is likely to be too high. The upper section of this canyon usually requires a couple of dry days prior to descent. There are small dams above the canyon.

38

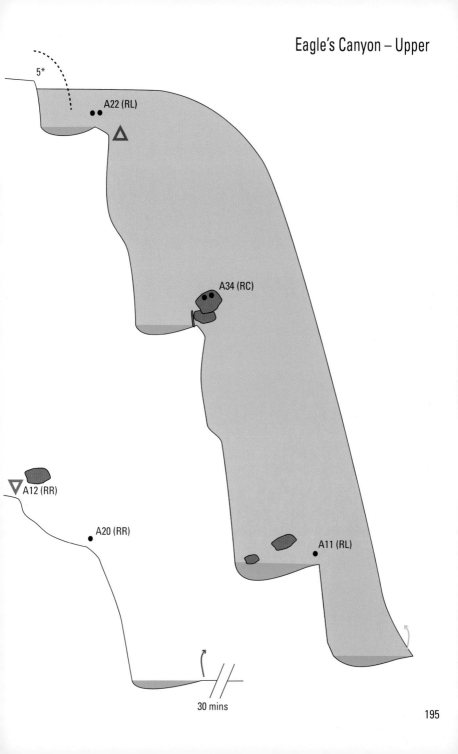

Eagle's Canyon – Upper

5*

A22 (RL)

A34 (RC)

A12 (RR)

A20 (RR)

A11 (RL)

30 mins

# Eagle's Canyon – Lower

| | |
|---|---|
| **Star rating** | ★★ |
| **Grade** | 4+ B/C |
| **River** | Eas an Tuirc |
| **Duration** | 1hr approach – 2hrs descent – 30mins return |
| **Canyon length** | 400m |
| **Longest abseil** | 55m |
| **Parking** | NN 193 128 (56.2729, -4.9192) |
| **In** | NN 221 145 (56.2895, -4.8759) |
| **Out** | NN 218 147 (56.2910, -4.8809) |

## Canyon description

The Black Linn is the name given on the OS map to this deep canyon. This is very apt, as it has carved its way down the hillside like a black scar. Enjoy an impressive start to this section of the canyon or make the long journey up to the fantastic upper section for a big canyon day.

## Getting there

Follow the same directions for Eagle's Canyon – Upper

## Approach

The approach is almost the same as the upper section except this time you continue a little further along the road past the pylons until you reach a patch of forestry on

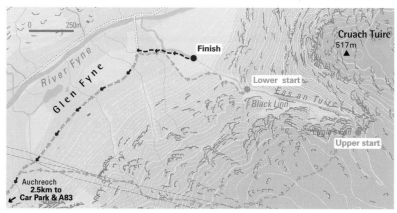

The big pitch

the right side. The canyon should be well in view now. Walk up the side of this forestry patch on the river-left side. You can either continue up the steep hillside river-left or cross over and walk up river-right, until you can see into the long gorge-walk section. You should be at a point you can easily climb down to the start of the lower section.

## Descent

Starting off with the big one, enjoy a long slanting abseil down into the black gorge below. You will be using a variety of natural anchors for the remainder of the canyon to descend down the multiple waterfalls below. There is one tricky jump to be discovered halfway down but it may contain a bit of debris.

The gorge eventually opens out as you enjoy some beautiful waterfalls down to an easy exit left. Walk along the riverside until you can cut through the forestry and back to the road. Now just begin the long walk back to the car.

## Water level marker

See details under Eagle Falls – Upper.

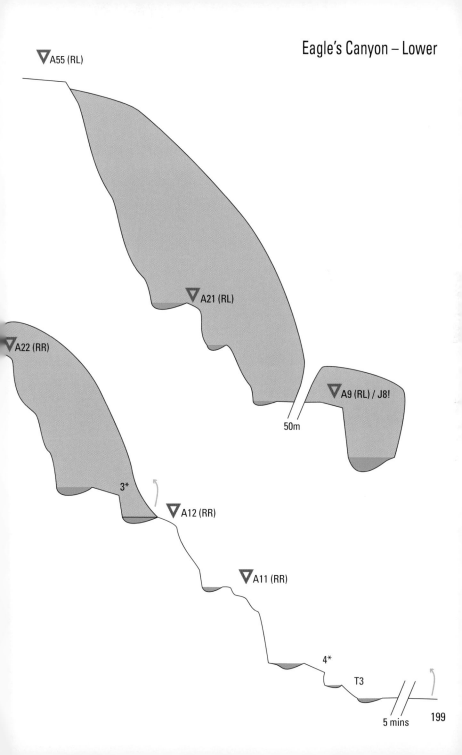

Eagle's Canyon – Lower

A55 (RL)

A21 (RL)

A22 (RR)

A9 (RL) / J8!

50m

3*

A12 (RR)

A11 (RR)

4*

T3

5 mins

199

Into the gorge

# Viaduct Gorge

| Star rating | ★★ |
| --- | --- |
| Grade | 3+ B |
| River | Dubh Eas |
| Duration | 25mins approach – 2 to 2.5hrs descent – 10mins return |
| Canyon length | 1.2 km |
| Longest abseil | 18m |
| Parking | NN 319 197 (56.3396, -4.7209) |
| In | NN 313 202 (56.3444, -4.7317) |
| Out | NN 318 200 (56.3430, -4.7226) |

## Canyon description

An interesting gorge tucked away up the back of Loch Lomond. This is a good place to explore when you are newer to the sport as the trickier sections can be avoided if necessary. For the daring there are a few deep pools for technical jumping.

## Getting there

Drive north on the A82 from Dumbarton until you reach Drovers Inn. No more than a mile north from the Drovers Inn there are a couple of options for parking. On the left is a road blocked by a gate where you can park one, maybe two cars without blocking the way. A little further past this is a small dirt layby on the right opposite a gravel track that passes over a cattle grid. You can park one car here.

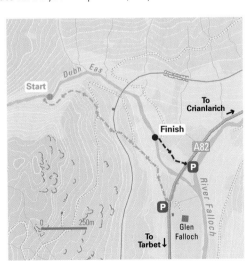

## Approach

To access the canyon, follow the road through the gate from the car parking spot on the river-right side. Follow this track uphill, keeping left at the first split. This road will cross over the railway then split again. Here you need to follow the right-hand track for a short while and when it starts to go downhill, look for a faint trail that follows the contours around the hillside – walk along this. Eventually a waterfall will come into sight and you will need to descend a grassy slope to gain access to the top of the waterfall.

## Descent

The first waterfall is simple to descend and starts your journey down towards the gorge. The next waterfall can be a bit trickier to rig for a clean retrieval but gives you a fun aquatic line. It is possible to avoid this abseil by climbing around river-right for a dry abseil or a daring jump once you've inspected where to land.

After this, some beautiful gorge-walking leads you to a couple of small un-rigged features before reaching another larger waterfall. There is a boulder blocking the exit of the pool below. The section below here may be dangerous to navigate in high flows. You can easily scramble along the river-right bank to an optional daring jump or simple abseil position.

There are a few more small features under the viaduct, then a long gorge-walk before eventually exiting up the bank on river-left. Walk down the gravel road leading back to your vehicle.

**40**

## Water level marker

You can check the flow from the road bridge near the parking area. This gorge could be descended in most flows but if a majority of the rocks in the river are fully covered it is too high and too dangerous to descend.

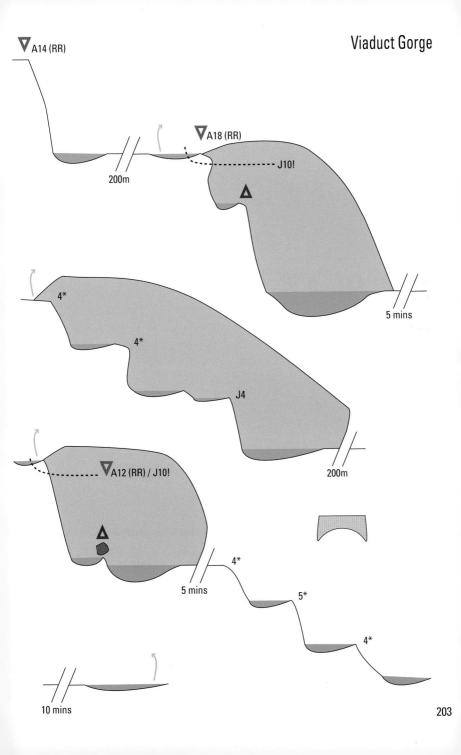

A14 (RR)

A18 (RR)

J10!

200m

5 mins

4*

4*

J4

200m

A12 (RR) / J10!

5 mins

4*

5*

4*

10 mins

Admiring the views

# Drovers Falls

| | |
|---|---|
| **Star rating** | ★★ |
| **Grade** | 4 A/B |
| **River** | Ben Glas Burn |
| **Duration** | 40mins approach – 3hrs descent – 5mins return |
| **Canyon length** | 800m |
| **Longest abseil** | 48m |
| **Parking** | NN 321 187 (56.3309, -4.7173) |
| **In** | NN 327 182 (56.3266, -4.7062) |
| **Out** | NN 321 186 (56.3300, -4.7158) |

## Canyon description

This spectacular canyon contains a huge waterfall, seen clearly from the Drovers Inn. Above the main attraction there is a variety of waterfalls that add to the interest or can be avoided if you so choose. For those looking for a big jump afterwards, the Falls of Falloch is just up the road.

## Getting there

**41**

Drive north up the A82 out of Dumbarton or south from Crianlarich. Just north of the Drovers Inn is a small turning over a bridge – signposted for Beinglas Farm Campsite. You can park here for a small fee, paid at the onsite shop.

## Approach

The steep approach track is located past the café area on the right. Walk past the outdoor seating, heading towards the play-ground at the back. Behind this you will see a steep muddy track that zigzags its way uphill. Follow this trail which climbs up the

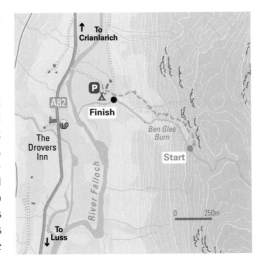

📷 Cruising down the rope

river-right side of the canyon. After a steep climb, some waterfalls will come into view beside a deer fence. This area is just a few pitches above the main waterfall and you can enter here if you so choose. Otherwise, continue uphill on the track, not along the fence-line! After about 15mins there will be an obvious entry point where a short grass bank leads down to the river.

## 41 Descent

The starting section is a simple gorge-walk until you reach a small but tight gorge, which can be avoided but has its interests. After this the river will eventually take a left turn and begin to get steeper. The open area of waterfalls here offer up the option to rig multiple abseils or downclimb the majority of them. When the largest pitch comes into view you can climb out left to a tree which is used to abseil down to the bolts safely. From this bolt station you can now enjoy the long abseil that brings you down onto a large ledge for another abseil. A short gorge-walk leads you down into the hidden gorge below where some interesting features and a final jump finishes off the descent.

When the river flattens out, take an obvious exit river-right which leads you back to the campsite. Now enjoy a warm cup of coffee.

## Water level marker

You can check the flow by looking at the large waterfall from Drovers Inn. If the waterfall looks broken like a spray of water, it is low flow and ideal. If the jet at the top is quite white, then it's medium and can be dangerous at the pitch-head. Any more water is too dangerous.

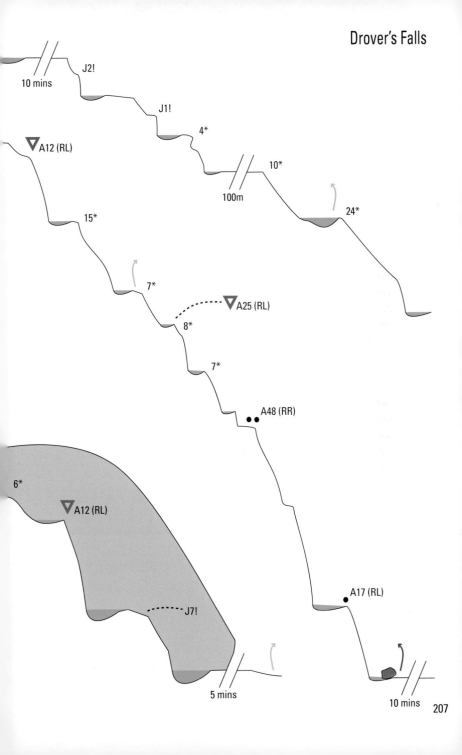

Mikey sliding down

# Falls of Barvick

| Star rating | ★★ |
|---|---|
| Grade | 3 A |
| River | Barvick Burn |
| Duration | 25mins approach – 1hr 30mins descent |
| Canyon length | 500m |
| Longest abseil | 20m |
| Parking | NN 849 243 (56.3967, -3.8653) |
| In | NN 850 248 (56.4013, -3.8644) |
| Out | NN 849 243 (56.3967, -3.8655) |

## Canyon description

A nice small canyon located just a few minutes' drive from Crieff, with fun little features and some low angle slides to enjoy. This is an easier canyon where you will find plenty of natural anchors or bolts in place where they are needed.
There may be a few more gorges to explore in this area.

## Getting there

**42**

Leaving from Crieff on the A85 towards Comrie, take the right turning towards the Famous Grouse distillery just outside the town. Drive past the distillery, resisting temptation, and follow the road right and then take a left where it splits. Follow this 10mph road around and stop where the road splits again just by a bridge. Park off the road here next to the bridge.

## Approach

The approach is simple. Start by following a faint trail up the river-left side of the gorge. Keep following this path until the river starts to flatten out. Get in around here where access is easy.

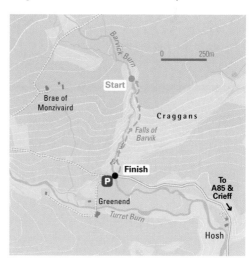

## Descent

Starting in a flat riverbed, begin walking downstream to the first feature. An abseil drops you into the gorge where you'll find some nice features that follow. In particular there is a steep-sided section of the gorge that you can walk around and back up into it, or find the jump down into it. Further down is a fun low-angled toboggan you can mess around on.

You'll know you're at the end of the canyon when you come upon the final curving abseil with the road in sight. Easy exit out back up to your vehicle.

## Water level marker

A simple one to check by just looking over bridge into the river. This canyon will go in all but very high flows. Only experienced canyoneers should attempt this canyon in higher flows. There is a small dam further upstream of the canyon to be aware of.

**42**

Final waterfall

# Mission Canyon

| | |
|---|---|
| **Star rating** | ★★ |
| **Grade** | 4 B/C |
| **River** | Cailness Burn |
| **Duration** | 2hrs approach – 3 to 4hrs descent – 1hr return |
| **Canyon length** | 800m |
| **Longest abseil** | 28m |
| **Parking A** | NN 327 054 (56.2115, -4.6998) |
| **Parking B** | NN 337 089 (56.2432, -4.6852) |
| **In** | NN 350 059 (56.2170, -4.6618) |
| **Out** | NN 342 062 (56.2195, -4.6754) |

## Canyon description

True to its name, Mission Canyon involves quite the journey to get to. But you are rewarded with an impressive descent down an untamed canyon that not many have visited before.

## Getting there

To kayak there – drive to Tarbet on the A82, north from Dumbarton or south from Crianlarich. Just out of Tarbet, heading towards Crianlarich on the A82, there is a large parking area up a left turn. Park up here (Parking A) or in the smaller layby opposite the turn on the Loch Lomond side.

To hike there – Drive to Aberfoyle and take the B829 to Inversnaid. After about 11 miles you will reach a T-junction, turn left to Inversnaid. Eventually you reach Inversnaid Hotel and you can park in the car park here (Parking B).

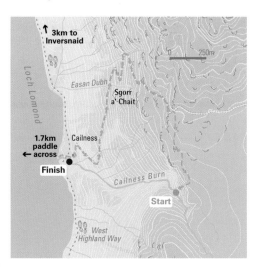

## Approach

Kayaking – This is why it's called Mission Canyon; you will now need to paddle across the loch to reach the canyon on the other side. The paddle across is roughly 1.7km from the parking area outside Tarbet over to Cailness. Once you reach the other side you should find the river flowing into the loch. There is a wooden bridge crossing the canyon at the bottom.

Hiking – From the Inversnaid Hotel, walk south along the West Highland Way for about 3km until you reach Cailness at the canyon's finish.

Just north of the river, begin hiking uphill on a trail beside the lonely house of Cailness. You should be following a steep 4x4 track that zigzags up the hillside on the river-right of the canyon. At the last left bend before the track heads away from the canyon and over the hill, veer off to the right over the peaty ground to the canyon you can see ahead of you. As you get close, you will descend into a small tributary that leads you down to the start of the canyon below a large broken waterfall.

## Descent

**43**

This adventurous canyon is made up of a multitude of interesting abseils. The start begins with a couple of simple abseils before gorge-walking along to a spectacular drop where the river turns sharp left. Below you can see into the stunning steep-sided gorge you will be descending into. Towards the end of this gorge, you will find one pitch with a bolt. This drop has been jumped from a ledge on the left and from halfway down off a slippery ledge, but the pool below may have shallowed out since then and will require checking first.

Some simple gorge-walking brings you down and out to Loch Lomond. From here you can now return by boat to Tarbet or hike back to the Inversnaid Hotel.

## Water level marker

Unfortunately, there is no way to check this canyon prior to getting there. It is best to get a gauge from the other rivers flowing in the area. This canyon has a decent catchment area off the back of Ben Lomond so ideally you will want to make the journey after a dry spell.

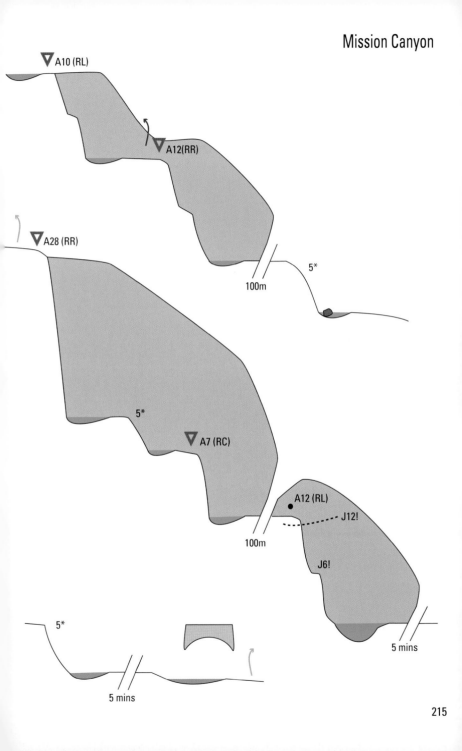

Mission Canyon

215

# Finlas Gorge

| Star rating | ★★ |
| --- | --- |
| Grade | 3 A/B |
| River | Finlas Water |
| Duration | 10mins approach – 1hr descent – 5mins return |
| Canyon length | 500m |
| Longest abseil | 18m |
| Parking | NS 352 882 (56.0584, -4.6486) |
| In | NS 346 882 (56.0579, -4.6567) |
| Out | NS 352 881 (56.0573, -4.6484) |

## Canyon description

A wonderful little gem of a gorge less than an hour's drive from Glasgow. Beautifully carved sandstone rock at the start and a jungle feeling gorge-walk afterwards. It's not overly complicated either, a brilliant simple descent.

## Getting there

**44**

Driving north from Dumbarton on the A82 you will need to turn left onto the A817, signposted for Garelochhead. Less than 100m up this road, on the left, is a layby. Park here. Do **not** park in the large layby further up the road on the right as this is a lorry escape lane.

## Approach

From the layby, walk uphill on the A817 until you reach the road bridge spanning the gorge. Either climb over the fence river-left to gain access to the canyon for the normal starting point, or climb over the fence river-right to walk underneath the bridge for the alternative start. **Caution** – The fences may be electrified.

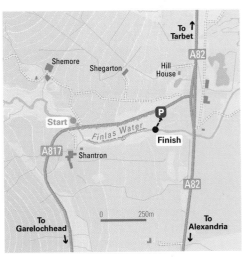

📷 Mind if I drop in?
– Andy T

44

## Descent

Starting in the canyon, you will find a natural anchor for descending the two-tier drop into the steep-sided gorge. A small tight drop below this may be tricky in high flows. The alternative start is a chain anchor from underneath the road bridge that allows you to avoid these first two features, useful for when the flow is higher. The remainder of the route leads you through a wild, fern-covered gorge with small features to overcome and one more abseil from bolts.

The gorge walls become steeper toward the end before opening up to an easy exit up the river-left bank. Cross through a field and walk back to your vehicle.

## Water level marker

You can assess the level of the water from the road bridge crossing the gorge at the start. If the flow of the first waterfall looks too pushy but not massive you can take the alternative start. If the waterfall looks dangerous and full of water, do not descend.

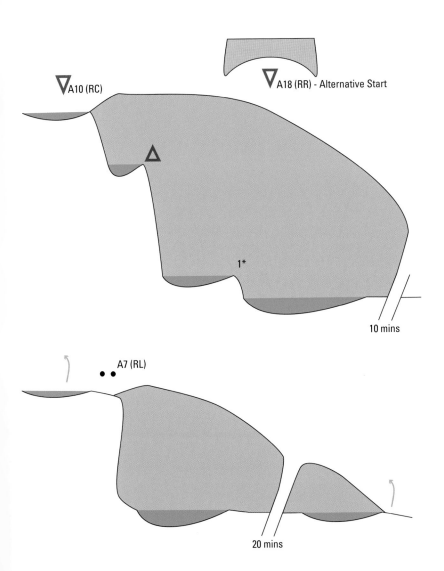

A10 (RC)

A18 (RR) - Alternative Start

1*

10 mins

A7 (RL)

20 mins

# Alva Glen Canyon

| | |
|---|---|
| **Star rating** | ★★★ |
| **Grade** | 4 B |
| **River** | Alva Burn |
| **Duration** | 45mins approach – 2hrs descent – 15min return |
| **Canyon length** | 650m |
| **Longest abseil** | 23m |
| **Parking** | NS 884 975 (56.1570, -3.7976) |
| **In** | NS 883 985 (56.1659, -3.8006) |
| **Finish** | NS 885 981 (56.1624, -3.7972) |
| **Lower finish** | NS 886 975 (56.1575, -3.7950) |

## Canyon description

This is a beautiful slot canyon, one of only a few slot canyons in Scotland. The steep rock walls create spectacular waterfalls, most of which only a canyoneer has the opportunity to see, making it a true hidden gem.

## Getting there

45

Drive to the town of Alva on the A91. As you drive down the main road through Alva, look for a turning north onto Brook St (it's a small road beside a red corner shop). Follow this road all the way, over a few crossroads, until you see a brown sign for Alva Glen. Head up this track to the car park.

## Approach

From the car park, follow the footpath uphill beside the burn and cross over the footbridge. Keep following the trail uphill with the river on your left side. Eventually you cross back over the burn, just

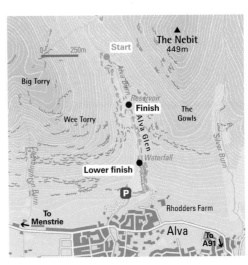

downstream of an old dam. This is your exit point from the canyon. Keep working your way uphill and the path will start to flatten out, leading to a viewpoint of a large cave-like feature on the stream. Follow the path around the hillside. You can either get in below the cave by heading down the grass slope or carry on around and get in above the cave where the burn flattens out.

## Descent

**45**

The first abseil above the cave mouth can be quite aquatic in normal flows and a bolt on the opposite wall can be found to set-up a guided abseil if needed. This then brings you out into an incredible amphitheatre of rock. Carry on gorge-walking from here to reach the next few small features. A tight slide further downstream may need a handline if there are strong flows as it's easy to get washed over the next abseil (bolts river-left). A tight passage brings you out to the top of a beautiful hidden twisting waterfall. One final abseil will bring you out of the main canyon and back to the dam. Exit river-right and walk back down the path.

There are some more features if you choose to carry on downstream. Eventually, you will walk through a deep gorge that leads to another dam. Abseil down the dam to finish at the first footbridge (lower finish). This section adds about 1 hour to the descent time.

## Water level marker

There is a dam just upstream of the first footbridge, not far from the car park. If there is water flowing over this in separate streams the canyon is at medium flow. However, if there is a single curtain of water flowing over the dam the canyon is at high flow and becomes very pushy in parts.

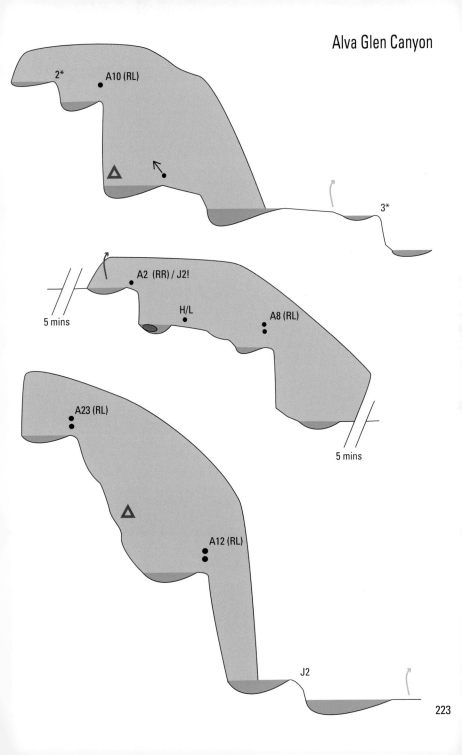

Alva Glen Canyon

# Dollar Canyon

| Star rating | ★★★ |
|---|---|
| Grade | 4 B |
| River | Dollar Burn |
| Duration | 40mins approach – 2 to 3hrs descent |
| Canyon length | 600m |
| Longest abseil | 17m |
| Parking | NS 964 989 (56.1719, -3.6704) |
| In | NS 959 995 (56.1770, -3.6786) |
| Out | NS 961 992 (56.1740, -3.6753) |

## Canyon description

A fantastic canyon surrounded by thick green moss and dense canopy giving it a fairy-tale feel. There are brilliant features all the way down the canyon including a spectacular two-tier waterfall. Popular with canyoning companies.

## Getting there

**46**

Drive to Dollar on the A91, not far from Alva. As you drive through the town on the main road you will see a small stream at the eastern side of town. Take a turn north next to a small clocktower, up the side of the stream. At the end of this road, turn right and then take the first left. Take the next left turn at a small brown sign for Castle Campbell. Follow this road up and take the right turn into the first car park you see and park here. Do not continue up the steeper road to the upper car park.

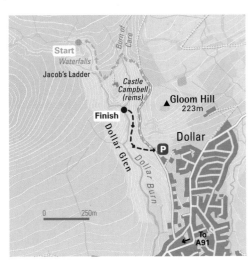

## Approach

Walk up the road towards the castle. As you reach Castle Campbell, take the path that turns off to the right and walk around the hillside, uphill alongside the canyon. You will be able to view into the canyon at points along the path. Keep heading up the track until you reach a small bridge spanning the gorges. Hop over the fence on the upstream side, river-left. Get in above the first feature.

## Descent

The descent starts with a great little slide into the first pool then on to some shallow interesting features under the bridge. The canyon opens a little for a short while after the bridge until you reach a feature where the water flows under an overhanging canyon wall, river-right. This was once a daring toboggan but has since filled up with silt. You can check it by scrambling / abseiling down river-left. Straight after this is the hidden two-tier waterfall. A handline may be in-situ at the second pitch, please leave in place for companies that run this trip. Some more scrambling and a few small jumps follow as you make your way down into the lower section. The final slot abseil station can be found by climbing out on the left and scrambling down to a wedged rock. This can be avoided by walking down left if you choose. The small jump straight after the abseil into the leaning slot is very shallow!

Once you turn a corner through a steep section, you will see your exit at the railed viewpoint. Follow the path that goes downstream and eventually take the path that goes up left back to the car park.

## Water level marker

There is a burn beside the road after you turn off the main A91 going through Dollar. This is a good indicator to what's happening in the canyon. Check the rocks in the riverbed; if most of the rocks are just covered the canyon is high. This canyon is very tight and can be very hydraulic in high flows.

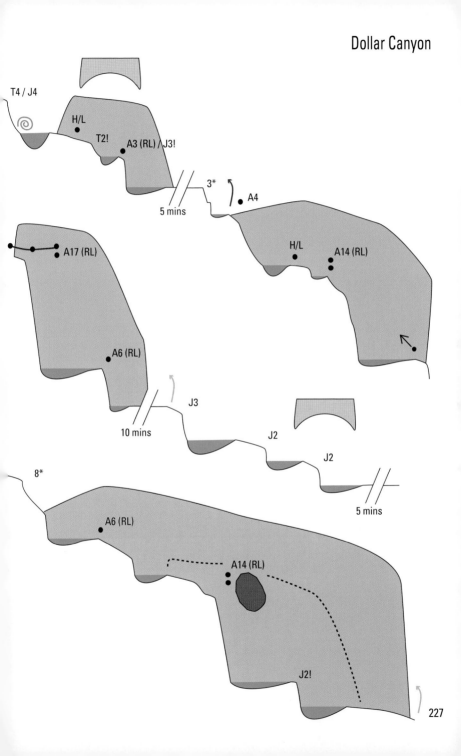

Dollar Canyon

T4 / J4

H/L

T2!

A3 (RL) / J3!

5 mins

3*

A4

A17 (RL)

H/L

A14 (RL)

A6 (RL)

10 mins

J3

J2

J2

5 mins

8*

A6 (RL)

A14 (RL)

J2!

227

Deep gorge w

# Rumbling Bridge

| Star rating | ★★ |
| --- | --- |
| Grade | 3+ B/C |
| River | River Devon |
| Duration | 15mins approach – 1hr descent – 15mins return |
| Canyon length | 650m |
| Longest abseil | 10m |
| Parking | NT 017 995 (56.1777, -3.5853) |
| In | NT 018 999 (56.1812, -3.5834) |
| Out | NT 016 994 (56.1768, -3.5862) |

## Canyon description

This canyon cuts incredibly deep into the landscape and is full of interesting gorge-walking. Viewing platforms along the river allow pedestrians to watch as you make your way through a maze of features. Debris in this river often creates dangerous siphons so take care in higher flows.

## Getting there

47

Driving north from Edinburgh on the M90, take the exit at junction 5. Turn left on the B9097 and follow this road all the way to Crook of Devon. At the junction, turn left onto the A977. Drive along this road until a right turn, signposted for Rumbling Bridge. Take this turn and drive through the village to an old stone bridge, crossing the gorge. Park in a layby beside this bridge.

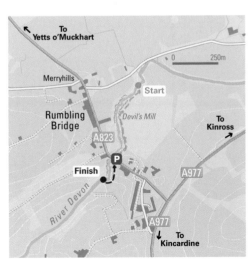

## Approach

Cross the bridge, then head through the gate beside the bridge on the river-left side. Follow the path along until the river starts to flatten out and is easy to access. Get in here at a calm pool.

## Descent

The first few small features require some downclimbing and may have debris blocking the flow. Simple to navigate gorge-walking eventually brings you to an awesome bridging section where the river squeezes through a very tight space before dropping into a deep pool. It is possible to bridge up to give yourself a small jump. Straight after this is a small waterfall that drops beside a viewing platform, which comes in handy for an anchor.

The canyon now starts to descend until upi reach its impressive deepest point, far below the road bridge. It is a spectacular place to be and you have a unique view of the old bridge still in place below the new one. Under the bridge, the river undercuts the rock and debris often makes this section difficult to pass, take great care in higher flows. Passing this, the canyon begins to open out as you climb down over large boulders.

When the river flattens, exit river-left and follow a faint trail along the fence back uphill to the layby.

## Water level marker

47

The water level can be checked as you walk up the trail. You will not want too much flow in this gorge. At the starting point the river should have very little flow. If it looks pushy then do not descend.

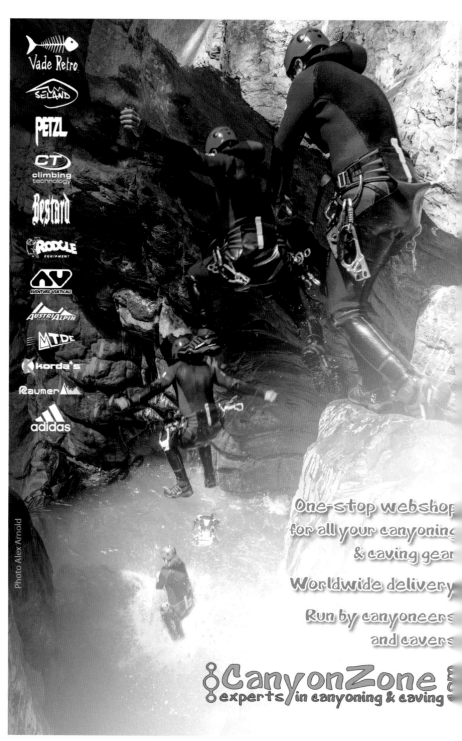

One-stop webshop
for all your canyoning
& caving gear

Worldwide delivery

Run by canyoneers
and cavers

§CanyonZone§
§experts in canyoning & caving§

# Glossary

**Anchor** – the object which you build your abseil from, i.e., bolts, tree, etc.

**Aquatic** – describing a feature to be very wet, generally with a strong current.

**Burn** – the Scottish term for stream.

**Catchment area** – the area in which precipitation is collected and fed towards the beginnings of the river.

**Downstream** – the direction going with the flow of the river.

**Flow** – another term for the current of water.

**Fall** - short for waterfall.

**Gorge-walk** – movement down a steep-sided stream which in most cases can be done both upstream and downstream.

**Guided rappel** – a form of abseil used to help avoid a hazard at the base of the waterfall.

**Loch** – a body of water, a lake or inland section of sea.

**Pitch** – a single rappel to reach either the bottom of a waterfall or down to the next abseil anchor.

**Re-belay** - also known as re-anchoring, is a method used to split long abseils or reposition an abseil to avoid hazards.

**River-right** – describing the right-hand side of the river as you look downstream.

**River-left** – describing the left-hand side of the river as you look downstream.

**Sliding abseil** – a forward facing abseil, sitting down in the sliding position.

**Slot** – a tight passage of the river with very steep sides, often inescapable.

**Upstream** – the direction going against the flow of the river.

# Other Routes

Below are a few popular waterfalls and gorges that have gradually become more of a tourist destination. Most of the information you'll need for these routes can be found on the internet with a quick search. Enjoy.

## Fairy Pools – Isle of Skye

Easily the most well known set of waterfalls in Scotland. They're easy to find and access, with the building of a new path. While it is a rather short route, it does offer up some interesting gorging in a beautiful area. There are few good jumps to discover and a beautiful natural archway to dive under.

## Corrieshalloch Gorge – Wester Ross

One of the deepest gorges around, containing an outstanding waterfall with great views from the suspension bridge that spans above it. While the waterfall itself hasn't been rigged yet for abseil, you can still have great fun exploring this gorge by simply gorge-walking up from the bottom (when the river is low). Just keep driving down the road towards Ullapool and find a spot to park where you can access the river below. You can explore all the way up to the base of Measach Falls.

## Black Spout – Pitlochry

Tucked in beside the bustling town of Pitlochry is a picturesque series of waterfalls, but you'll need a big rope for this route. It's more of a one-hit wonder with only the main waterfall being the attraction but there is a some gorge-walking above and below it to be done. A short trip overall but why not when it's so close to town. You can always check it out first from the lovely viewpoint.

## Soldier's Leap (Killiecrankie Gorge) – Killiecrankie

A popular spot for those who like a big jump! This small section of gorge isn't a route per se but more of a classic cliff-jumping spot. Head to the National Trust visitor centre and park here. A short walk down to the various sizes of cliff jumps. This spot was made famous by the Redcoat soldier who once leapt across the raging River Garry to escape pursuing Highlanders.

The biggest jump you'll find here is around 15m!

### Falls of Falloch – Loch Lomond

Well-known amongst kayakers for being a brilliant waterfall to run, but it's also a brilliant jump. Simply park in the well-signposted car park then make your way above the waterfall. There is a small gorge up above this main fall with a few small features to find before you reach the top of the falls. People who go here for the jump tend to use the take-off point on river-right, giving you a clean 11m drop. A good spot to go to if you've been canyoning in the area.

### Devil's Pulpit (Finnich Glen) – Glasgow

Once a quiet gorge-walk now a popular tourist destination after being featured in films and TV series. Easy to access but my advice would be to visit here early in the morning, the parking can be horrendous (this may change). This is a beautiful deep gorge with red-tinted water flowing through the amazing carved rock. A lovely simple gorge walk to enjoy.

# New Canyons / Gorges

*Discovered a new route for canyoning or gorge-walking?*

*Want to share this information with the rest of the canyoning community?*

Email - scottishcanyons@outloook.com with any of the following information and we will look at adding this route to any future guides and maps.

**Location** – get in/out grid references.

**Duration** – approach and descent times.

**Photos** – The more the merrier and as high a resolution as posssible.

Be sure to check out the UKCA website on www.ukcanyoning.org for any updates on new routes or existing routes that have changed. You also will find helpful information and location maps to the existing canyon routes in Scotland and the rest of the UK.

# Index of Place Names

## A

## B

## C

## D

## E

## F

## G

# UK CANYONING
# ASSOCIATION

## Standards, Development, Certification

The UKCA is a non-profit organisation recognised as the National Awarding and Training Body for canyoning and gorge walking activities throughout the UK.

The UKCA provides high quality, standardised, internationally recognised training and certification. UKCA training and certification courses are designed for all canyoneers from recreational through to professional level. Our training courses are all standardised following training standards set out by professional experts.

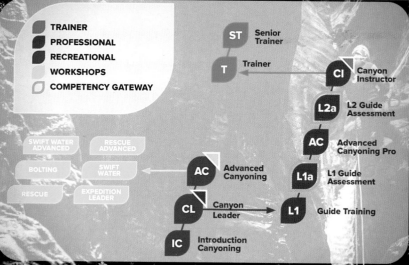

**TRAINER**
**PROFESSIONAL**
**RECREATIONAL**
**WORKSHOPS**
**COMPETENCY GATEWAY**

ST — Senior Trainer
T — Trainer
CI — Canyon Instructor
L2a — L2 Guide Assessment
AC — Advanced Canyoning Pro
L1a — L1 Guide Assessment
L1 — Guide Training

SWIFT WATER ADVANCED
RESCUE ADVANCED
BOLTING
SWIFT WATER
RESCUE
EXPEDITION LEADER

AC — Advanced Canyoning
CL — Canyon Leader
IC — Introduction Canyoning

For more information about training courses, certification or membership contact one of the current UK training centres, or the UKCA website.

**THE CANYONING COMPANY**

The Canyoning Company
Dunkeld, Perthshire
info@thecanyoningcompany.co.uk
07725813729

outdoor safety
TRAINING / CONSULTING / RESCUE

Outdoor Safety Training
Kinlochleven, Fort William
info@outdoorsafety.co.uk
07843 391922

admin@ukcanyoning.org
www.ukcanyoning.org

Photo: Charlotte Workman
Location: Dundonnell Canyon